max science primary

Workbook 4

DISCOVERING THROUGH ENQUIRY

SUNETRA BERRY

SERIES EDITOR: **BOB KIBBLE**

macmillan education

INTERNATIONAL CURRICULUM

Macmillan Education
4 Crinan Street
London N1 9XW
A division of Springer Nature Limited

Companies and representatives throughout the world

Workbook ISBN 978-1-380-02164-9

First published 2019

Original design by EMC Design Ltd and Macmillan Education
Page make-up by Ink Design
Illustrated by Nick L'Ange, Deevine Design, Chris Venter, Bev Victor, Sean Strydom, Natalie and Tamsin Hinrichsen, Marna Hattingh
Natalie and Tamsin Hinrichsen pp 6, 121, 123, 124; Nick L'Ange pp 17, 38, 48, 69, 122; Deevine Design pp 8; Chris Venter pp 9, 10, 57, 58, 59, 61, 77, 84; Bev Victor pp 39, 40, 51; Sean Strydom pp 32, 101 (bottom), 102, 104, 105, 106, 107, 108; MAC Archive pp 31; Marna Hattingh pp 111
Cover design by Sparks Publishing Services Ltd and Macmillan Education
Cover illustration by Star Publishing Pte Ltd and Jorge Santillan c/o Beehive Illustration Agency
Picture research by Susannah Jayes

The author and publishers would like to thank the following for permission to reproduce their photographs:
Getty Images/johnaudrey p22(D), Getty Images/C Squared Studios p117(triangle), Getty Images/Clive Nichols p70, Getty Images/YinYang p117(drum); **Shutterstock**/Rostilsav Ageev p22(E), Shutterstock/Bezzangi p62, Shutterstock/mohd kamaul hafiz p56 (bar magnet), Shutterstock/JIANG HONGYAN p22(F), Shutterstock/eNjoy iStyle p117(maracas), Shutterstock/mrotchka p117(thumb piano), Shutterstock/schankz p22(C), Shutterstock/Alen Thien p22(B), Shutterstock/Virunja p22(A), Shutterstock/yurcehello108 p56 (ring magnet); **Stockbyte** pp56 (horseshoe magnet), 117 (violin).

Printed and bound in India
2023 2022 2021 2020 2019
10 9 8 7 6 5 4 3 2

Contents

Introducing the *Max Science primary* Workbook

The **Max Science primary Workbooks** accompany the **Student Book** for class and home use. All the numbered activities and extension activities found in the Student Book are expanded with clear answer spaces and support. Instructions carefully show if activities are to be done independently, in pairs or in groups.

Practising my science language

Supported activities focus on improving scientific literacy to make the learning of science through the medium of English more accessible.

Extending understanding

Extension questions encourage learners to go a bit further to improve the depth of understanding.

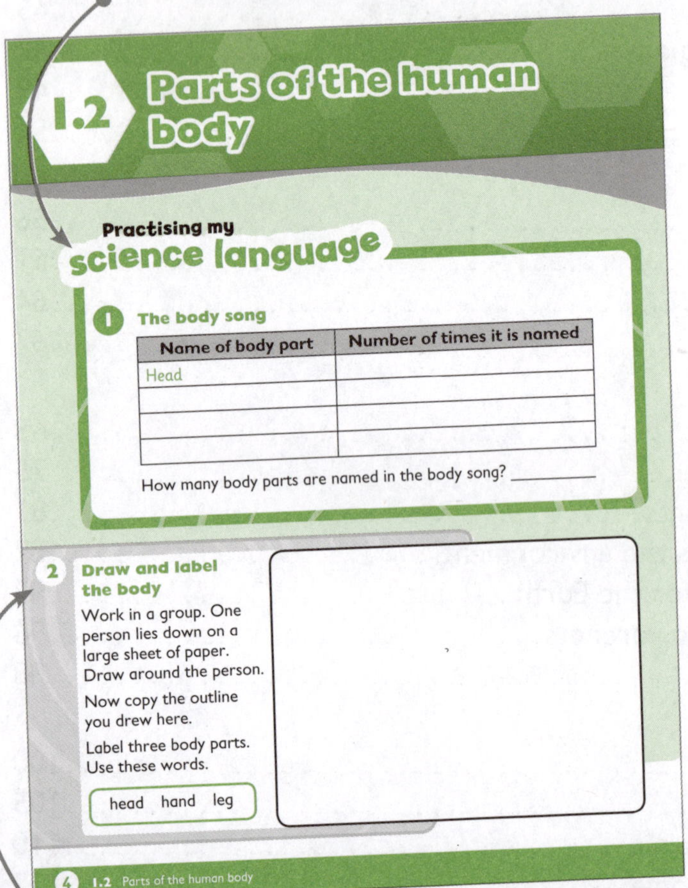

1.2 Parts of the human body

Practising my **science language**

1 The body song

Name of body part	Number of times it is named
Head	

How many body parts are named in the body song? ______

2 Draw and label the body

Work in a group. One person lies down on a large sheet of paper. Draw around the person.

Now copy the outline you drew here.

Label three body parts. Use these words.

head hand leg

4 1.2 Parts of the human body

Extension

Look at the picture. Why is the toy a non-living thing?

I think it is a non-living thing because it

Checklist

Read each sentence and circle a face for it. Like this:

I understand.

I understand a bit.

I need more help to understand this.

- I can say if something is alive.
- I know the differences between living and non-living things.
- I can name some living and non-living things.

38 1.2 Parts of the human body

Exploring science further

Numbered activities from the Student Book are expanded with example answers for guidance. Learners can record their scientific progress, insights and results.

Assessing progress

End of topic checklists provide opportunities for recording what learners have learnt so far.

1.1 Skeletons

1 Drawing the dinosaurs

a. Look at the picture of a dinosaur skeleton on page 3 of the Student Book. What do you think it looked like when it was alive? Discuss your ideas with your partner.

b. Now draw a picture to show your idea.

Extension

Look at some more pictures of dinosaur skeletons. What clues do skeletons give about how dinosaurs lived?

___

___

___

2 Investigating bones

Get into groups. Your teacher will give you some bones.

a. What do the bones look like?

- Use a magnifying glass to look closely at the bones.
- Draw some of the bones.

Bone 1	Bone 2	Bone 3

b. What do the bones feel like?

- Circle words that describe the bones.

hard soft smooth rough knobbly round long thin thick

- Write one more word here: ______________________

c. Choose one of the bones. What part of the animal do you think it comes from? What gives you this idea?

I think that bone ___ comes from ______________________

because it is ______________________

______________________.

3 Bones and fingers

a. Touch your fingers. What can you feel under the skin? ____________

b. Bend your fingers. How many bones are there in each finger?

Thumb: _______

Index finger: _______

Middle finger: _______

Ring finger: _______

Little finger: _______

c. Draw what you think your finger skeleton looks like.

4 Getting an X-ray image

Work in a group.

Imagine someone in your group has broken their arm. They need to have an X-ray image taken.

Role play what will happen when they go to hospital.

- One of you needs to be the patient.
- One of you needs to be the radiographer.
- Some of you need to be other health workers, for example, a doctor or a nurse.
- Some of you can be the patient's family.

Who played the different parts?

__________________ was the __________________.

__________________ was the __________________.

__________________ was the __________________.

__________________ was the __________________.

__________________ was the __________________.

1.2 The human skeleton

1 Muddled skeleton

Hakim has tried to label a skeleton, but he has made some mistakes.

Cross out the incorrect labels and write the correct labels in the spaces. Use the words in the box.

An example has been done for you.

shin wrist finger
spine ankle rib
toe thigh bone
neck arm

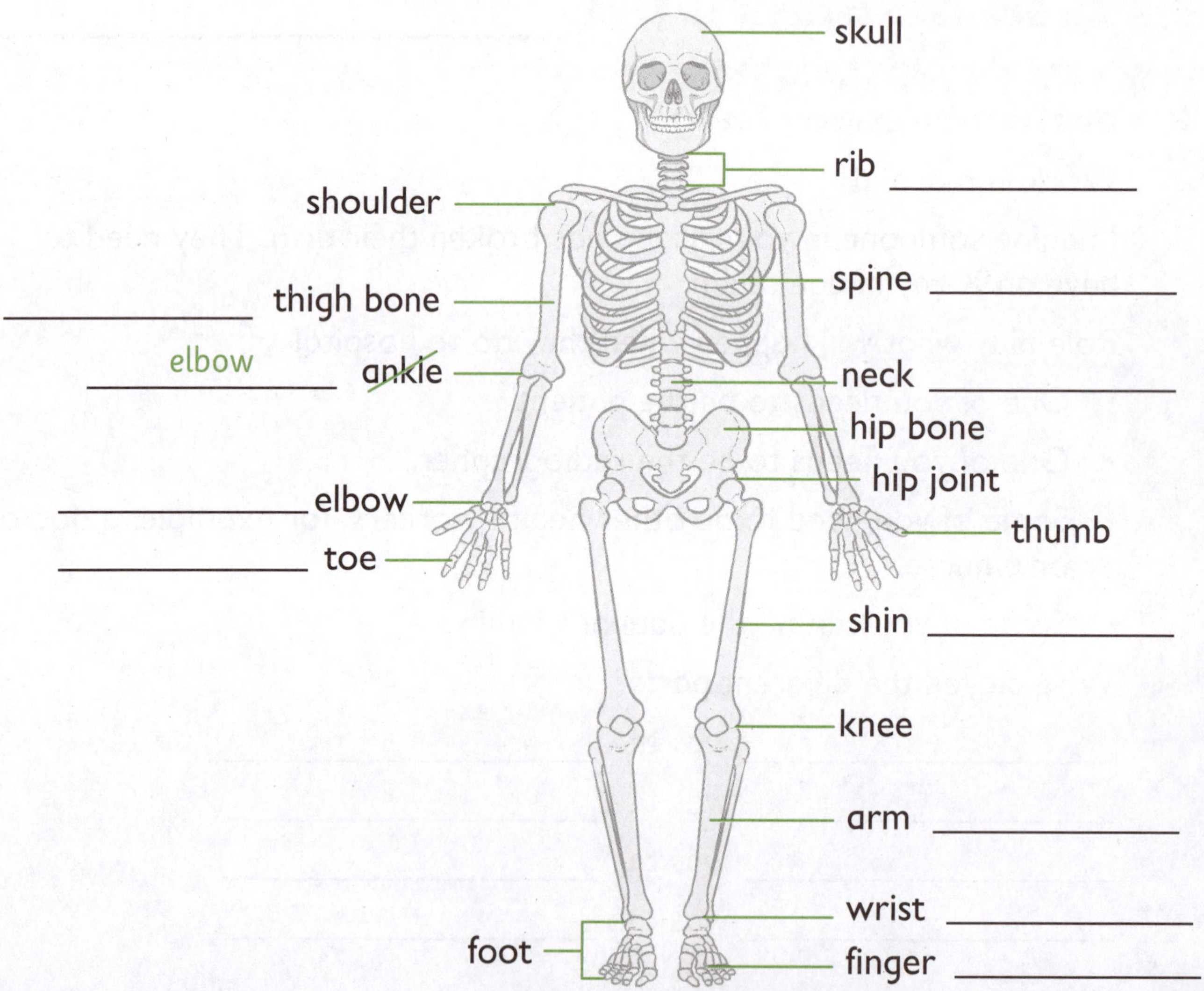

Extension

a. How does the skeleton protect the brain, heart and lungs? ____________________

____

____

____

Hint

Think about how a shell protects an egg, or how a cage keeps a bird safe.

b. Why do the brain, heart and lungs need protection?

____

____

____

Practising my science language

spine skull
elbow ribs
hip bone shoulder
neck wrist knee

2 What jobs does the skeleton do?

a. Search for these bones hidden among the letters. Circle each one you find.

s	b	a	n	e	c	k	d	l	e
h	p	l	d	n	q	c	h	i	l
o	s	k	u	l	l	o	i	t	b
u	p	f	y	b	u	j	p	z	o
l	i	v	s	r	h	p	b	k	w
d	n	w	r	i	s	t	o	n	h
e	e	e	m	b	p	x	n	e	r
r	k	t	q	s	f	a	e	e	m

b. Write down two bones for each of these jobs:

- Support: ____________________
- Protection: ____________________
- Movement: ____________________

1.3 Do skeletons grow?

1 Investigating bone lengths

Work with a partner.

a. Measure your arm, from your elbow to your wrist, in centimetres. Use a ruler.

Write down the length. ________ cm

b. Is your arm bone the same length as other people's bones?

- Talk to three other people in your class. Find out how long the bone in their lower arm is. Record the measurements in the table.

Name of person	Length of lower arm (cm)

- Now ask your teacher to measure their own arm.
Write the measurement here. ________ cm

c. Look at all the measurements in the class. What pattern can you see?

____

____

____

Extension

a. Ask some adults and younger children if you can measure their bones.

- Choose three different bones to measure. Write the names of the bones in the column headings.
- Measure these bones in each person.
- Record the person's age and bone lengths in the table.

Age of person (years)	Length of ________ (cm)	Length of ________ (cm)	Length of ________ (cm)

b. What can you learn from your measurements? ____________________

____

____

c. Can you use your measurements as evidence that bones can grow?

Yes **No**

Why do you say so? Describe any patterns that you see in your results. ____________________

____

2 Drawing a bar chart

Here are some measurements of people's arm lengths at different ages.

Person	Length of arm (cm)
Toddler	15
Young child	20
Older child	25
Teenager	30
Young adult	35
Middle-aged adult	35

a. Complete the bar chart to display these measurements. The bar for the toddler has been drawn to help you. Add the bars for the other people.

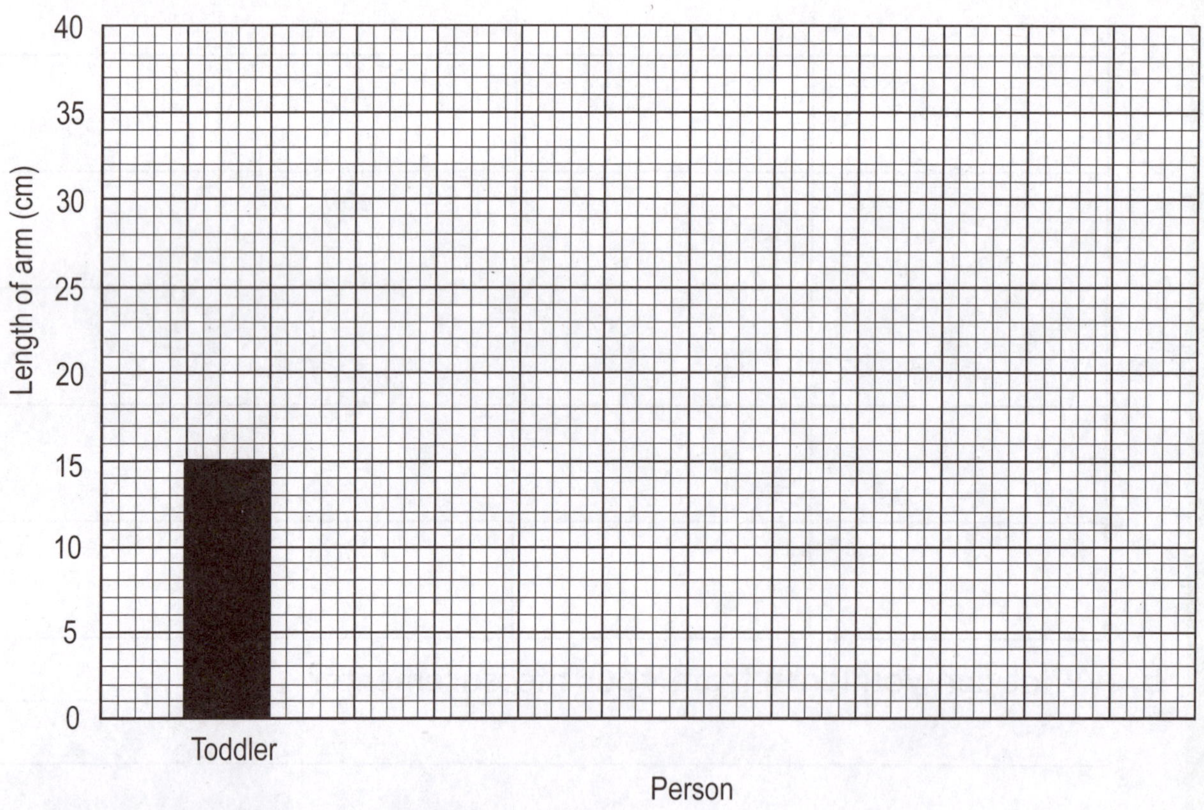

b. Is there a trend? Explain your answer. ______________________

____

c. What conclusions can you make? ______________________

____

Extension

a. At what age do you think our bones stop growing?

I think our bones stop growing when ______________________________

____.

b. Why is it important that our bones stop growing at some stage?

Talk to your partner. Write down your ideas. ____________________

____

Extension

Matin is 40 years old.

a. Which thigh bone belongs to him? Tick your answer.

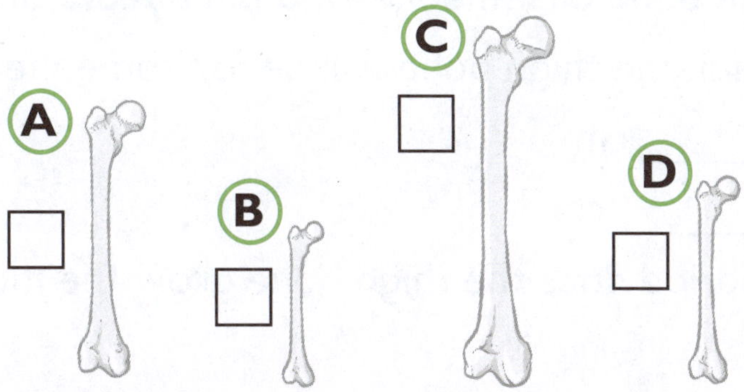

b. Draw the bones in order of people's ages.

- Write the letter of each bone next to it.

Baby	Toddler	Teenager	Adult

- Describe the pattern you see. ______________________________

____

3 Growth of the human thigh bone

Look at the chart. It shows the average length of the thigh bone at different ages.

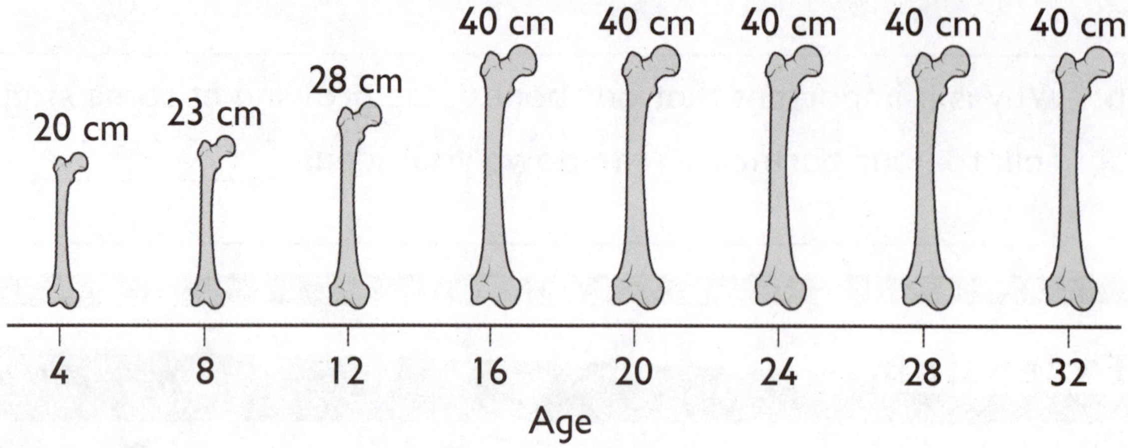

Use the chart to answer the following questions.

a. How long is the thigh bone of someone who is 12 years old? ______ cm

b. How long do you think the thigh bone will be for someone who is:

- 9 years old? ________ cm
- 40 years old? ________ cm

c. In which four-year period does the thigh bone grow the most? Circle your answer.

4–8 years **8–12 years** **12–16 years** **16–20 years**

d. Describe the general trend you can see in the results.

____

____

____

____

____

____

____

____

Checklist

- I understand.
- I understand a bit.
- I need more help to understand this.

Read each sentence and circle a face for it. Like this:

- I know that our skeleton consists of many different bones.
- I know that X-ray images can show us how our bones look.
- I know what the three jobs of my skeleton are.
- I can name parts of the human skeleton.
- I know that my bones grow with my body and can heal if they break.

1.4 What are medicines?

1 Treatments for symptoms

Look at the symptoms people have when they are unwell.

Choose the best way to help someone in each case.

One answer has been done for you.

Symptoms	Ways to help people feel better
Cold and shivery	Cool them down with a damp cloth.
Hot and sweaty	Give them plenty of hot drinks and cough syrup.
Headache	Wrap a blanket around them.
Thirsty	Give them plenty of water to drink and let them sleep.
Sore throat	Give them plenty of water to drink.

2 Which medicine?

Your teacher will show you different medicines.

a. Which of these medicines have you taken?

____

continues on following page ...

b. Why did you take the medicine? What were your symptoms?

I took the medicine because ______________________________

______________________________.

My symptoms included ______________________________

______________________________.

c. Which other medicines have you taken before? ______________

____

Practising my

science language

3 Be safe with medicines

Here is an information leaflet about a medicine called aspirin.

Medicine = Aspirin

Used for: Headaches, symptoms of cold and flu, fever, sore throat, toothache

Contains: Aspirin

Warning: Do not give to children under 16 years old, unless advised by a doctor.

How to take: Take 1 to 3 tablets every 4 hours. Do not take more than 12 tablets in 24 hours.

Do not take aspirin if you:

- have stomach ulcers
- are younger than 16
- are allergic to aspirin or any substances included.

Each tablet contains: 300 mg aspirin, maize starch, talc, lemon flavour and sweetener.

continues on following page …

... continued from previous page

a. Why is it important to read the information leaflet for a medicine carefully? ______________________

____

____

b. Use the leaflet to answer the following questions:

- How old do you have to be to take aspirin? ________ years
- How much aspirin is in each tablet? ________ mg
- Name one thing that taking this medicine will help with.

  ____
- How much of this medicine can you take in 24 hours?

  ________ tablets

Extension

The label on a bottle of a cough medicine for children says:

Children aged 6–12 years: Take 2.5 ml (½ teaspoon) twice a day. **Do not take more than 5 ml (1 teaspoon) in 24 hours.**

Jacob is 8 years old. He has a cough. His mother gave him 2.5 ml of medicine at 10 o'clock in the morning.

At 5 o'clock in the afternoon, Jacob is still feeling unwell. Can his mother give him more medicine? ______________________

____

4 School rules for anyone feeling unwell

a. What rules does your school have for anyone feeling unwell? Ask your school nurse or your teacher. Write down the rules.

____

____

____

b. What do you suggest to improve these rules?

____

____

Checklist

I understand.

I understand a bit.

I need more help to understand this.

Read each sentence and circle a face for it. Like this:

- I know that there are different types of medicine.
- I know that medicine can help to make us better when we are ill.
- I know that all medicines can be dangerous if taken incorrectly.
- I can say what kind of information is given in an information leaflet.
- I know that children may take medicine only when an adult is present.

1.5 Movement, bones and muscles

1 Moving in different ways

Work with your partner. Take it in turns to stand up and move different parts of your body.

a. Describe which bones or joints you are using in each movement.

An example has been done for you.

- When I bend my arm, my elbow moves.
- When I nod my head, ______________________________
  ______________________________.
- When I wiggle my toes, ______________________________
  ______________________________.
- When I make circles with my arms, ______________________________
  ______________________________.
- When I turn my leg at my hip, ______________________________
  ______________________________.

b. How do you think your muscles help you to move?

____

____

____

____

2 How do bones move?

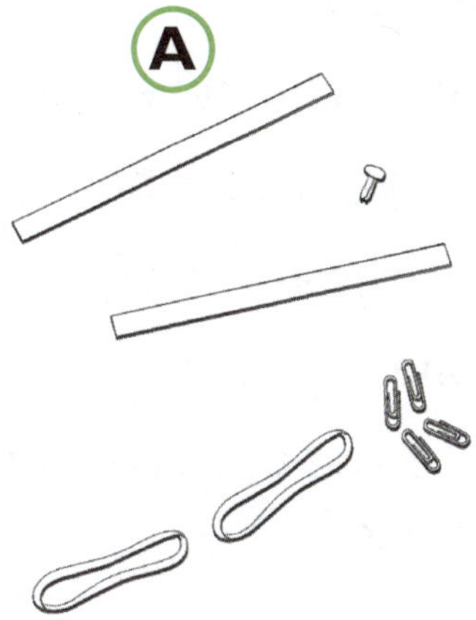

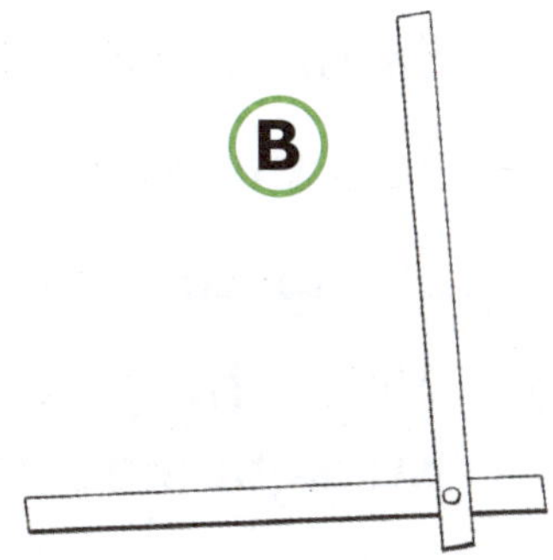

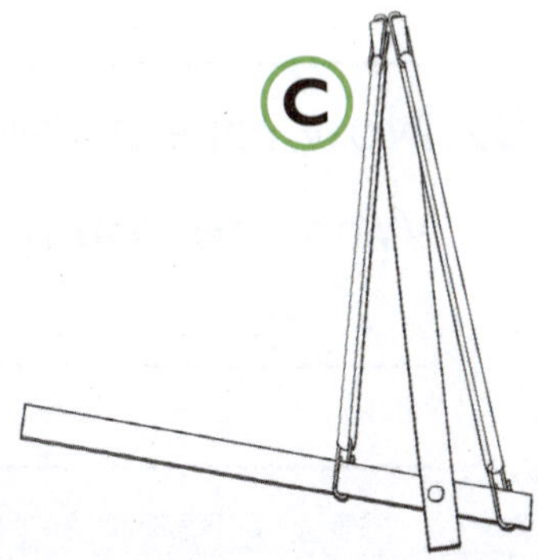

Your teacher will show you a video about how your muscles and bones work together.

a. Make a model to show how your arm muscles and elbow let you move your arm.

Follow these instructions.

A Cut two lengths of cardboard. They should be 5 cm wide and 30 cm long. These represent the bones in your arm.

B Push a split pin through one end of each piece of cardboard. Fasten the cardboard strips together by opening the ends of the split pin.

C Use large paper clips to attach two rubber bands to the cardboard strips.

b. Describe how the model works.

- Which part of the arm does the split pin represent? ____________
- What happens to each elastic band when you move the piece of cardboard that represents the lower arm?

  ____

  ____
- How is your model different from a real arm?

  ____

  ____

Hint

Muscles cannot become longer. They can only become shorter when they contract and return to their original length when they relax.

3 Exploring leg muscles

Do the following where you have plenty of space around you:

- Sit on a chair, with your legs bent at the knee.
- Feel the muscles in the front of your thighs.
- Straighten your one leg at the knee, extending your lower leg upwards.

a. What happened to the muscles in the front of your thigh as you straightened your leg?

____

____

b. Now repeat the movement, but feel the muscles in the back of your thigh. What do you notice?

____

____

Extension

You have learnt about bones and muscles. How do they work together? Complete these sentences. Use the words in the box to help you.

bones	pairs	relaxes	move

Your muscles work in ______________. Muscles are connected to your ______________. When one muscle contracts, the other muscle in the pair ______________. This causes the bone to ______________.

Practising my

science language

4 Investigating muscles

Jack and Bill are weight lifters. Jack has big muscles. He says he is stronger than Bill.

Plan a fair test to see if Jack is right. Work in pairs.

a. What are the variables in the test? ______________________________

____

____

b. Which factor will you change? ______________________________

____

c. What will you measure? ______________________________

____

d. What apparatus or equipment will you need? ______________________________

____

Checklist

Read each sentence and circle a face for it. Like this:

I understand.

I understand a bit.

I need more help to understand this.

- I know that muscles are attached to my skeleton.
- I can describe how muscles work in pairs to make my bones move.
- I can describe how muscles relax and contract.

1.6 Other types of skeleton

Practising my science language

Safety

Be careful when handling invertebrates. They are animals and must be respected.

1 Observing invertebrates

a. Go on a tour around your school grounds. Look for some invertebrates.

- Look in the soil or under stones.
- Wear gloves. Collect a sample of invertebrates.

b. Use a magnifying glass to observe the invertebrates. Record your observations below.

- Choose two of the invertebrates you collected. Then answer the questions for each one.
- Draw a picture of each invertebrate. Write its name.

Invertebrate 1: ______________	**Invertebrate 2:** ______________

continues on following page …

... continued from previous page

- How well is the inside of each invertebrate protected? Tick your answer.

Invertebrate 1: Not well at all ☐ A little bit ☐ Very well ☐

Invertebrate 2: Not well at all ☐ A little bit ☐ Very well ☐

- How does the invertebrate move? What part of its body does it use to move? Complete the sentences using words from the box.

wings	legs	fly	jump	crawl	hop	walk	swim	glide

Invertebrate 1 uses its ________________ to ________________.

Invertebrate 2 uses its ________________ to ________________.

- Are there any other features that can help the invertebrate to move or protect itself?

Invertebrate 1: ________________________________

____

Invertebrate 2: ________________________________

____

2 Which type of skeleton?

What kind of skeletons can you see in the photos on the following page? Which animals are:

- vertebrates? ________________________
- invertebrates with an exoskeleton? ________________________
- invertebrates without a skeleton? A ________________________

continues on following page ...

… continued from previous page

Write the correct letter(s) next to each question. An example has been done for you.

A

jellyfish

B

tree frog

C

worm

D

scorpion

E

lobster

F

rabbit

3 Designing your own invertebrate

a. Describe what your invertebrate animal looks like.

- What is its outside skeleton like? ______________________
- Describe the invertebrate's shape. ______________________
- What colour is the invertebrate? ______________________

b. Draw this new invertebrate.

continues on following page …

... continued from previous page

c. What are the advantages of an exoskeleton? What are the disadvantages? Talk about it in your group and complete the sentences below.

An exoskeleton helps the animal ______________________________

____.

An exoskeleton makes it harder for the animal to ________________

____.

Hint

Think about protection and growth and movement. How does an exoskeleton help an animal like a crab? How does it make things harder?

Extension

Find out more about an invertebrate animal.

- How does it move?
- What gives its body support?
- How does it protect its softer parts?

Prepare a short talk for your class.

Checklist

Read each sentence and circle a face for it. Like this:

- I understand.
- I understand a bit.
- I need more help to understand this.

- I know what the difference is between a vertebrate and an invertebrate animal.
- I can name some vertebrate and invertebrate animals.
- I can compare different types of skeleton.

Glossary

In your own language, write down what these words mean.

animal

ankle

arm

bones

contract

cure

elbow

feet

fingers

fracture

hip

human

invertebrate

knee

medicine

move

Glossary

muscles

neck

relax

ribs

shin

shoulders

skeleton

skull

spine

symptoms

thigh

thumbs

vertebrae

vertebrate

wrist

X-ray

2.1 Comparing solids, liquids and gases

Practising my science language

1 Features of solids, liquids and gases

Complete the sentences to describe water in its three states.

Choose words from the list and add some words of your own.

hard	cold	runny	thin	wispy	hot	wet	misty

Ice is ______________ and ______________ and ______________.

Water is ______________ and ______________ and ______________.

Steam is ______________ and ______________ and ______________.

2 Exploring the properties of solids, liquids and gases

Your teacher will give you some materials.

Work in a group.

a. Investigate the properties of solids, liquids and gases.

- Feel each material.
- Try to squeeze the material when it is in a plastic bag.
- Pour each material into a tall, thin container. Then pour it into a short, wide container.

continues on following page ...

... continued from previous page

b. Record your observations here.

Use words from the box to complete the sentences. You can use a word only once.

shape	mix	hold	easy	keep	hard	container
spread	smaller	flows	difficult	bigger	pour	lose

Properties of solids

- A solid will __________ its shape even when it is not in a __________.
- Some solids are __________, but others are soft.
- It is __________ to squeeze a solid into a smaller space.

Properties of liquids

- A liquid does not have a fixed __________. It takes the shape of the container it is in.
- If I __________ a liquid out, it __________ to another spot.

Properties of gases

- I cannot __________ a gas in my hands.
- I can squeeze the gas inside a balloon into a __________ space.
- A gas can __________ with the air and __________ out around us.

3 Finding solids, liquids and gases

Look at materials around the classroom.

Are they solids, liquids or gases? Write their names in the correct column.

Solid	Liquid	Gas

2.2 The particle model

1 Acting out a particle model for a solid

Imagine you are a particle in a solid.

a. Work in a group to act out the particle model for a solid.

How do you all stay together? ______________________________

____

b. Use your model to describe the shape of a solid.

- What happens when another group tries to pull your group apart?

  ____

- What happens when another group tries to squeeze your group together more? ______________________________

  ____

c. Does your model fit your observations of actual solid materials?

Yes **No**

Explain your answer. ______________________________

____

2 Acting out a particle model for a liquid

Imagine you are a particle in a liquid.

a. Work in a group to act out the particle model for a liquid.

Hint

Remember that the particles in a liquid are always in contact with one another, but they can move around slowly.

continues on following page …

... continued from previous page

b. Use your model to compare how particles behave in a liquid and a solid.

- *If there is no container, the particles in a liquid* ____.
- *If there is no container, the particles in a solid* ____.

c. Ask another group to try to squeeze your group closer together.

How much closer can you all squeeze together? Tick your answer.

We cannot squeeze together at all. ☐

We can squeeze together a bit more. ☐

We can squeeze together much more. ☐

Extension

Drip some milk onto a plate. Then drip some honey in the same way.

a. Are they both liquids? Why do you say so?

____

____

b. Predict what will happen if you warm up the honey. Try to explain your answer using what you know about the particle model for liquids. ____

____

3 Acting out a particle model for a gas

Get into groups once more.

a. Imagine you are a particle in a gas. Act out the particle model for a gas in your group.

continues on following page ...

... continued from previous page

b. How is your model for a gas different from that of a solid or a liquid?

- Ask another group to try to squeeze your group closer together. What happens?

  We can squeeze together **a lot** / **only a little bit** / **not at all**.

- Does your gas model have a fixed shape? **Yes** **No**

  Why do you say so? ____________________

  ____

- If the classroom door was open, could any gas particles move out of the classroom? **Yes** **No**

  How is this different from a liquid or a solid?

  If the classroom door was left open, the particles in a solid would

  ____________________.

  If the classroom door was left open, the particles in a liquid would

  ____________________.

4 Comparing particle models for solids, liquids and gases

a. Draw a line to match each statement with the correct model, to compare solids, liquids and gases. An example has been done for you.

Statement		Model
The particles are spread far apart.		Solid
The particles are very closely packed in a regular pattern.		
The particles do not move around, but just vibrate.		Liquid
The particles are all touching, but they do not have a regular pattern.		
The particles move very fast.		Gas
The particles move slowly.		

continues on following page ...

… continued from previous page

b. Draw diagrams of the particle models for solids, liquids and gases.

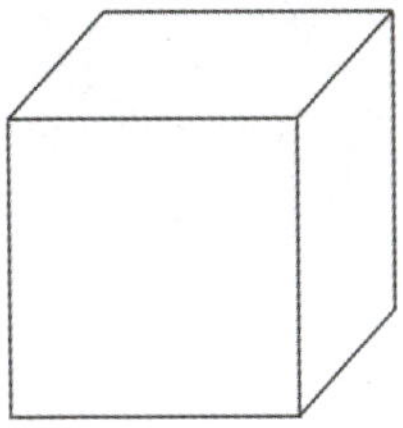

wood

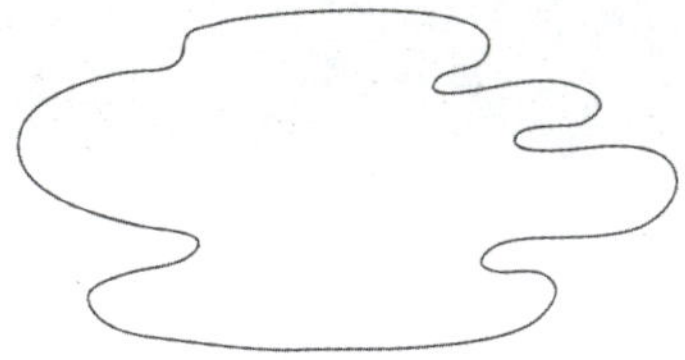

water

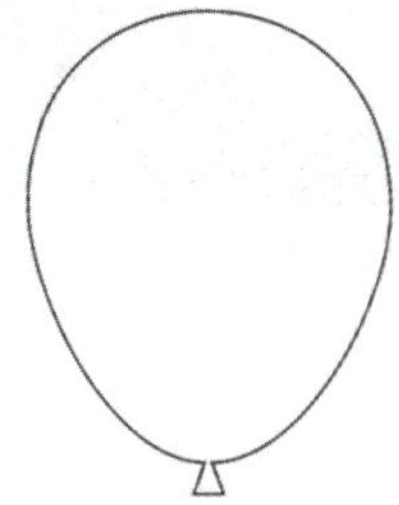

air

Checklist

Read each sentence and circle a face for it. Like this:

I understand.

I understand a bit.

I need more help to understand this.

- I can recognise solids, liquids and gases around me.
- I can describe the properties of solids, liquids and gases.
- I can describe how the particles in a solid, liquid and gas are arranged and how they behave.

2.3 Investigating liquids

1 Finding the runniest liquids

Get into groups. Your teacher will give you different liquids:

water PVA glue shower gel oil washing-up liquid

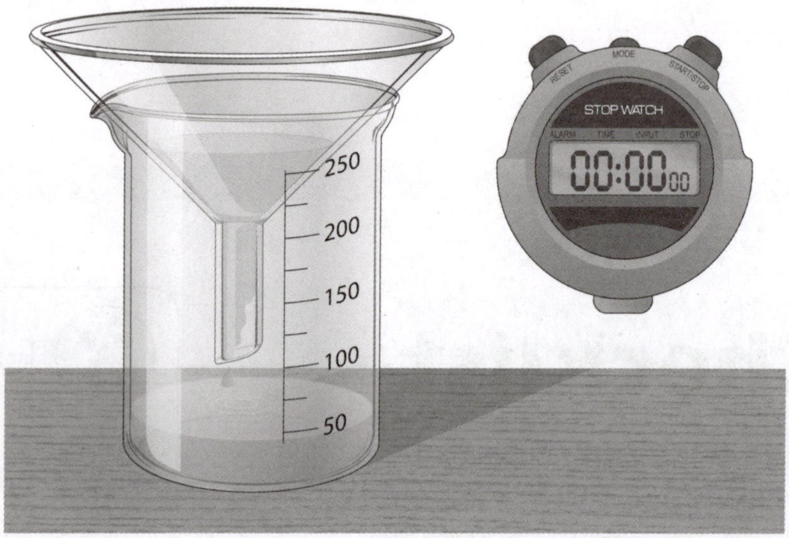

a. Plan an investigation using the equipment in the picture to find out how fast each liquid flows.

- Decide how to make it a fair test.
- What will you measure in your investigation?

Write your ideas here.

To make it a fair test, we will ______________________________

____.

We will measure ______________________________________.

continues on following page …

... continued from previous page

Write the steps of your investigation here. Number each step.

b. Draw up a table to record your results.

- Which factor are you changing? Circle your answer. Write this in the first column.

  time type of liquid type of container

- Which factor are you measuring? Circle your answer. Write this in the second column.

  time type of liquid type of container

______ (the factor being changed)	______ (the factor being measured)

continues on following page ...

... continued from previous page

c. Show your teacher your plan.

- Then carry out your investigation.
- Record your results in the table. Make sure you include the correct units for any measurements.

d. Present your results as a chart. Use this grid.

Type of liquid

- Which liquid is the thickest? ______________________________
- Which liquid is the thinnest? ______________________________
- Now look at your chart.

  What trend do you see? Circle the right word.

The thicker a liquid, the **faster** / **slower** it flows.

2 Investigating pouring

Your teacher will give you a cup of sand and a cup of water.

a. Pour the water onto a dish. Then pour the sand onto another dish. Observe what happens and talk to your partner about it.

b. How is sand like a liquid? ______________________

____

Why do you think this is? ______________________

____

Why is sand still a solid, even though it behaves like a liquid?

____

____

c. Predict what will happen if you repeat this with a cup of rice.

____

____

Checklist

- I understand.
- I understand a bit.
- I need more help to understand this.

Read each sentence and circle a face for it. Like this:

- I can name some liquids that flow easily and some that do not.
- I can describe an investigation to measure how fast liquids flow.
- I can recognise that some solids are unusual and appear to flow.

2.4 Investigating gases

Practising my science language

1 Looking for signs of gases

How can you see gases? Do the following tests.

Discuss your observations with your partner before you write about them.

a. Take a sponge and squeeze it hard under water. What do you see?

____

____

b. Blow up a balloon.

- How has it changed?

  ____

  ____

- What is inside the balloon now?

  ____

  ____

- If you could weigh the balloon before and after you blow it up, what would you expect to find?

  ____

  ____

continues on following page …

... continued from previous page

c. Blow into some water with a straw.

- What happens to the water?

  ____

- Explain your observations.

  ____

  ____

  ____

d. Stand in front of a fan.

What do you feel? Why can you feel this?

____

____

e. Watch as your teacher pours a certain gas onto a candle.

- What happens?

  ____

  ____

- What does this tell you about the gas?

  ____

  ____

  ____

2 Making a gas

Get into groups.

a. Follow these steps to make and collect a gas called carbon dioxide.

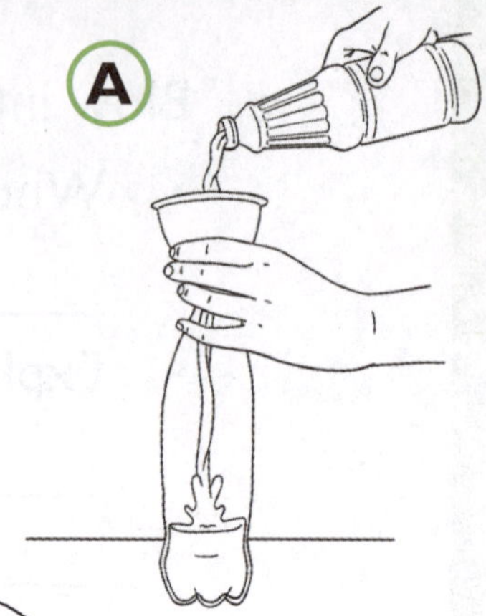

- Using a funnel, pour 100 ml of vinegar into an empty plastic bottle.
- Take an empty balloon and half fill it with baking soda.

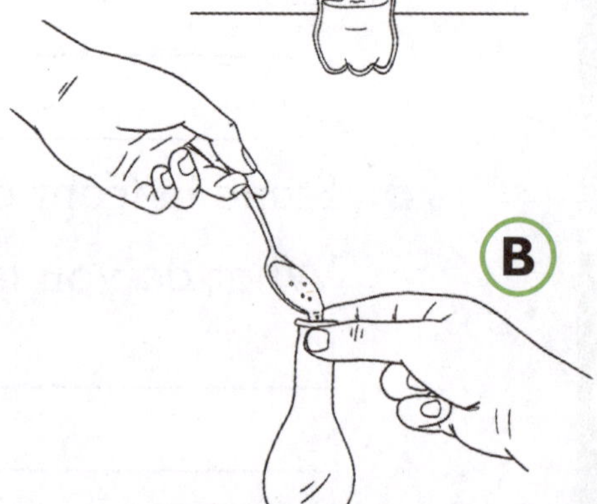

- Carefully place the open end of the balloon over the mouth of the bottle. Do not let any baking soda get into the bottle. Make sure the balloon completely covers the mouth of the bottle. You may need help with this.
- When your teacher has checked your bottle, empty the baking soda from the balloon into the vinegar.

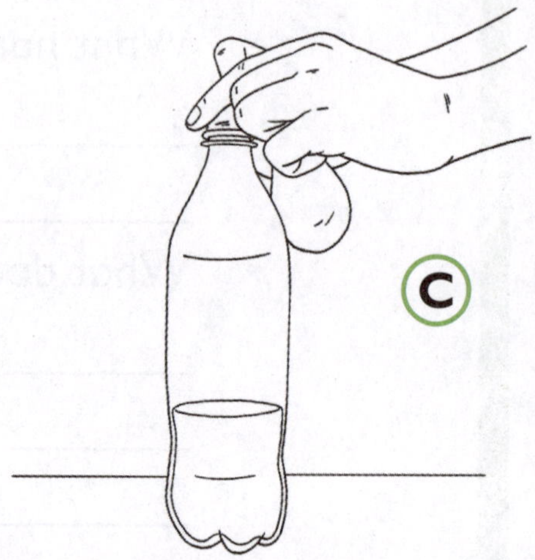

b. Complete the paragraph to record your observations. Use words from the box.

baking soda	fizzing	vinegar	
bubbles	inflate	gas	carbon dioxide

When the ____________ ____________ mixed with the ____________, we could see it ____________. There were lots of ____________. The balloon started to ____________. This is because a ____________ was given off.

This gas is called ____________ ____________ .

Extension

Over time the balloon will get smaller. What do you think has happened to the gas inside? How do you think this happened?

____

____

3 Testing a gas

Get into groups again.

a. Follow these instructions to test the gas you made in Activity 2.

- Watch as your teacher shows you how to remove the balloon from the bottle without losing any gas.
- Place your balloon inside a container.
- Carefully open the balloon and let the gas fill the container.
- Cover the container with a lid.
- Turn the container over and hold it close to the candle flame.
- Remove the lid.

b. What happened? Write your observations here.

____

____

4 Making carbon dioxide with yeast

Work in pairs. Your teacher will give you some yeast, sugar and other equipment.

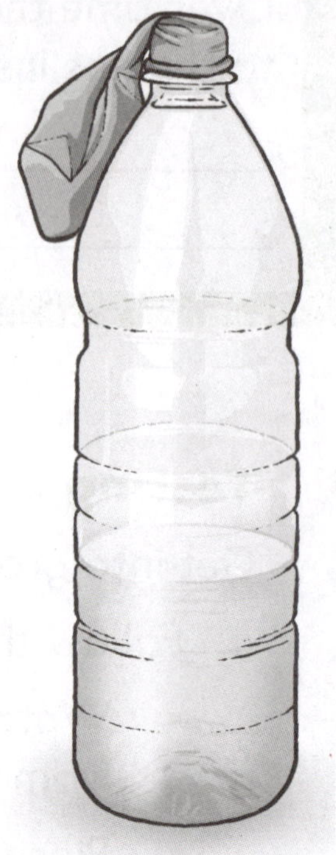

a. Follow these instructions to make a gas.

- Pour a small amount of warm water into the bottle.
- Add the yeast to the water in the bottle. Swirl it around.
- Now add all the sugar. Swirl it around and let it dissolve.
- Stretch the open end of the balloon over the mouth of the bottle. There should not be any gaps.
- Leave the bottle in a warm place.

b. What do you observe?

After some time ______________________________

____.

c. Test the gas in the same way as in Activity 3. How do you know the gas is carbon dioxide?

I know the gas is carbon dioxide because ______________________________

____.

Extension

Find out what increases the amount of carbon dioxide produced by yeast.

____

____

5 Making bubbles

Get into groups.

a. Follow these instructions to make bubbles.

- Use some washing-up liquid, shampoo or liquid soap.
- Add some thick sugar solution, glycerine or corn syrup.
- Add some water.
- Bend a pipe cleaner into a loop.
- Dip the loop into the soap mixture. Take it out and blow through the loop to make bubbles.

b. Try to make really big bubbles and others that last a long time.

- To make really big bubbles, we ______________________________
  ____.
- To make bubbles last a long time, we ___________________________
  ____.

Checklist

Read each sentence and circle a face for it. Like this:

I understand.

I understand a bit.

I need more help to understand this.

- I can name some gases.
- I can describe two ways to make carbon dioxide.
- I can describe two properties of carbon dioxide.

2.5 Melting

1 Investigating melting

Work in pairs. Your teacher will give you a beaker of ice cubes and a bowl of warm water.

a. Observe the conditions at the start of your investigation.

- How does the bowl of water feel? **Warm** **Cold**
- How does the beaker of ice feel? **Warm** **Cold**
- Draw the ice cubes in the beaker.

b. What do you think will happen when you put the beaker of ice in the bowl of water?

I predict that ______________________________

____.

continues on following page ...

… continued from previous page

c. Now put the beaker of ice in the bowl of water. What happens to the ice cubes?

- Draw a picture of the ice cubes after 10 minutes.

- Feel the bowl of water again. Is it warmer or colder than at the start of the investigation? Circle your answer.

  Warmer **Colder**

d. What can you conclude from this investigation?

____

____

____

Extension

Where in your classroom do you think ice cubes will melt very fast? Give a reason for your answer.

____

____

Practising my science language

2 Exploring how different solids melt

Work with your group.

Your teacher will give you: three foil cases, a bowl of warm water and three solids.

a. How will you set up your investigation?

- Draw a picture of each solid before you start your investigation.
- What will you do with the foil cases?

____

____

b. Record how long it takes for each solid to melt.

- Did all the substances melt at the same time? **Yes** **No**
- Write the time taken for each solid to melt here:

butter _______ candle wax _______ chocolate _______

c. What did you find out about melting solids? Complete the paragraph using words from the box.

heated	less	faster	time	particles	break	move	energy

Some solids melt _______ than others. This suggests that the _______ are not held together equally tightly in all solids. When the solids are _______, the particles gain _______. They eventually _______ free from each other and start to _______ around. In some solids the particles need _______ energy to break free than in others. This is why they do not all melt at the same _______.

2.6 Freezing

1 Freezing liquids

Your teacher will give you different liquids and an ice cube tray.

Investigate whether the liquids will freeze in the same time.

- Carefully pour each liquid into a space in the tray.
- Place the tray in a freezer.

Check the liquids 20 minutes, 40 minutes and 60 minutes after you put the tray in the freezer.

Record your results each time. Write down the names of the liquids.

Liquid 1: ____________

After 20 minutes, the liquid ____.

After 40 minutes, the liquid ____.

After 60 minutes, the liquid ____.

Liquid 2: ____________

After 20 minutes, the liquid ____.

After 40 minutes, the liquid ____.

After 60 minutes, the liquid ____.

Liquid 3: ____________

After 20 minutes, the liquid ____.

After 40 minutes, the liquid ____.

After 60 minutes, the liquid ____.

2 Exploring melting and freezing

Make a chocolate fruit stick.

- Your teacher will melt some chocolate.
- Dip fruit on a stick into the melted chocolate. Lay it on a tray.
- Place the tray in the freezer for 10 minutes.

How did the chocolate change in this activity? ______________________

____

Extension

Research three other uses of melting and freezing in the home or in industry. Give a description of each use on a separate piece of paper.

Checklist

I understand.

I understand a bit.

I need more help to understand this.

Read each sentence and circle a face for it. Like this:

- I can describe how to melt a solid.
- I can describe the changes to a solid as it melts.
- I know that freezing is the reverse of melting.
- I can describe the changes to a substance as it freezes.
- I can describe some uses of melting and freezing.

2.7 Heating liquids and cooling gases

Practising my science language

1 What happens when you breathe on a mirror?

Breathe on a mirror and then answer the questions below. Use the words in the box to help you.

warm	air	cools	condenses	droplets	lungs
surface	gas particles	lose energy	slow		

a. What do you see on the mirror?

____

____

____

b. Why do you think this happens?

____

____

____

2 Boiling and condensing water

Look at the diagrams below. They show water changing state.

- Which diagram shows cooling?
- Which diagram shows heating?

Label each diagram correctly.

_______________________ _______________________

Checklist

Read each sentence and circle a face for it. Like this:

- I understand.
- I understand a bit.
- I need more help to understand this.

- I can describe what happens when a liquid boils.
- I know that cooling a gas will change it back to a liquid.
- I can recognise when a liquid is boiling and when a gas is cooling.

2.8 Changes of state

Practising my science language

1 Identifying changes of state

Watch a video clip of a volcano erupting.

a. Talk to your partner about the different changes of state you see.

b. These sentences describe what is happening when a volcano erupts. Fill in the missing words. Choose words from the box:

liquid	cools	freezes	solid	melts	flows

- Rocks are solid.
- The rock ____________ deep inside the Earth where it is very hot. The solid rock turns into a ____________ called lava.
- The lava comes out of the top of the volcano. It ___________ down the slope. The lava ____________ as it hits the air, which is colder than inside the volcano.
- The lava ____________ and becomes a ____________.

2 Changing state and changing back

Work with your partner.

a. Plan an experiment to investigate how you can change ice to liquid water and then to gas, and all the way back again to ice.

- What equipment will you use? ______________________________

  ____

  ____

- Write out the steps you will follow. Say which states are involved.

  ____

  ____

  ____

  ____

  ____

- Draw pictures to show what you will do.

b. Show your plan to your teacher. Then carry out your investigation.

- Write about any observations.
- Suggest ways you could improve your method.

  ____

  ____

  ____

3 Reading a thermometer

Look at the pictures. Read the temperature on each thermometer.

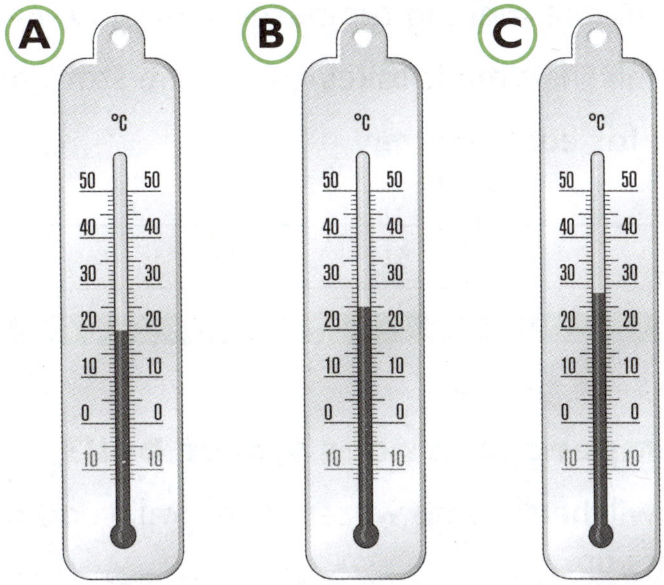

For each question, circle your answer.

- Which thermometer reads 28 °C? **A B C**
- Which thermometer reads 20 °C? **A B C**
- Which thermometer reads 25 °C? **A B C**

4 At what temperature does ice melt?

Your teacher will give you a beaker of ice.

- Measure the temperature of the ice. Write the temperature in the first row of the table.
- Place the beaker in a bowl of warm water.
- Measure and record the temperature of the ice every 30 seconds until it has all melted. Write your results in the table.

Time (s)	Temperature (°C)	Time (s)	Temperature (°C)
0		120	
30		150	
60		180	
90		210	

Extension

How might your results be different if you used a different amount of ice?

a. Do you think the melting temperature will be different?

b. Do you think the time it takes to change state might be different?

Give a reason for each answer.

____

____

5 At what temperature does water boil?

Your teacher will heat some water. They will read out the temperature as the water heats up.

a. Describe your observations.

- What happens to the temperature?

  ____

- What is happening to the particles of water?

  ____

b. The water will begin to boil.

At what temperature does water boil? ________ °C.

Extension

a. Find out the boiling and melting temperatures of three different substances. Fill in the table.

Substance	Boiling temperature (°C)	Melting temperature (°C)

continues on following page …

... continued from previous page

b. Why are the melting point and boiling point of a substance not the same? Think about what is happening to the particles during melting and boiling. Write your ideas here.

____

____

____

____

____

____

Checklist

I understand.

I understand a bit.

I need more help to understand this.

Read each sentence and circle a face for it. Like this:

- I can describe all the changes that occur when solids, liquids and gases are heated and cooled.
- I can use a thermometer correctly to measure temperature.
- I know the temperature at which ice melts.
- I know the temperature at which water boils.

Glossary

In your own language, write down what these words mean:

boil

bubbles

condense

cool

drip

evaporation

flow

freeze, freezing

gas

heat

liquid

matter

melt

model

particles

pour

Glossary

powder

reversible

solid

temperature

thermometer

water vapour

3.1 Properties of magnets

1 Exploring magnets

Get into groups. Your teacher will give you some magnets and other materials.

a. Which magnet is which? Draw a line to match each magnet with the correct picture. An example has been done for you.

- bar magnet
- horseshoe magnet
- wand magnet
- floating magnet

b. Test each magnet with the materials your teacher gave you. Do all the magnets work in the same way? **Yes** **No**

Explain why you say so. ______________________________

c. Now choose one magnet. Walk around your classroom and test the magnet on different objects. Which objects are magnetic and which are non-magnetic?

Write your answers in the table. An example has been done for you.

Magnetic objects	Non-magnetic objects
coin	plastic ruler

2 Attraction and repulsion

Get into pairs. Your teacher will give you two bar magnets.

- Let one bar magnet hang freely, as in the diagram.
- Bring each end of the other magnet in turn towards one end of the magnet in the sling.
- Do the same thing again but this time, take the magnet to the other end of the magnet in the sling.

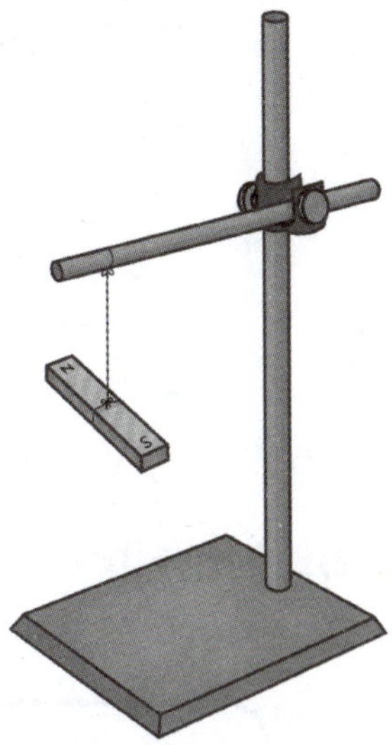

Record your observations.

a. When do the magnets attract each other?

____

____

b. When do the magnets repel each other?

____

____

3 Comparing different magnets

Get into pairs. Your teacher will give you some magnets.

a. Take two magnets that look the same. Draw them here.

continues on following page …

... continued from previous page

- Bring the two magnets towards each other. What do you observe?

  When I bring the two north poles together, ______________________

  ____.

  When I bring a north pole towards a south pole, __________________

  ____.

b. Now take two magnets that do not look the same. Draw the two magnets here.

- Bring the two magnets towards each other. What do you observe?

  When I bring the two north poles together, ______________________

  ____.

  When I bring a north pole towards a south pole, __________________

  ____.

c. What can you conclude about magnets?

- Do all magnets follow the same rules? **Yes** **No**
- Do some magnets show a stronger attraction than others? **Yes** **No**
- Do some magnets show a stronger repulsion? **Yes** **No**
- How hard is it to pull the magnets apart when they attract? Circle your answer.

  Very hard **Somewhat hard** **Not hard at all**

Practising my

science language

4 Explaining how magnets work

How do you think floating magnets work?

a. Label the poles of each magnet in the three diagrams.

b. Complete the sentences to explain how each diagram works.

Choose words from the box. You can use some words more than once.

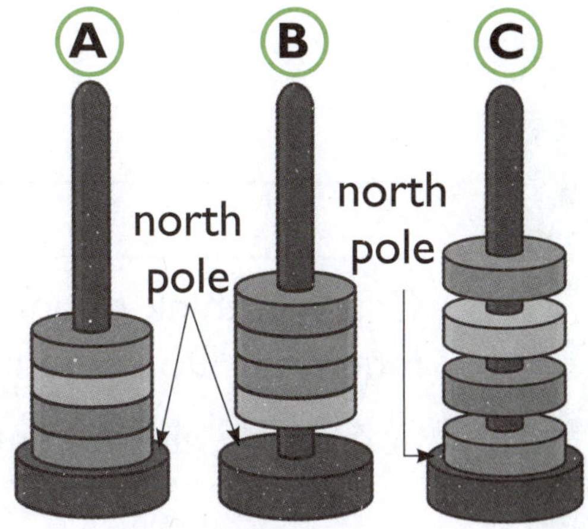

floating	north	repel	attracted	same	south

The black stand is magnetic. The top of the base is a north pole.

- In diagram A, the ring magnets are __________ to the base. If the top of the base is a north pole, the bottoms of the ring magnets must be __________ poles. This means the top of each ring magnet is a __________ pole.
- In diagram B, the ring magnets are __________ above the base. This is because the bottoms of the ring magnets and the top of the base __________. If the top of the base is a north pole, the bottom of each ring magnet must be a __________ pole.
- In diagram C, the bottom ring magnet is __________ to the base. The three other ring magnets are __________. This is because their poles __________ each other. They must be the __________ poles.

Extension

a. What have you learnt about magnets so far? Prepare a short talk to communicate your ideas. Write some notes here.

b. Can you think of another question you would like to ask about magnets? Do some research to find the answer to this question.

Something else I want to know about magnets is ______________________________.

After some research, I found out that ______________________________.

Checklist

Read each sentence and circle a face for it. Like this:

- I understand.
- I understand a bit.
- I need more help to understand this.

- I can name four magnetic metals.
- I can recognise magnets of different shapes.
- I know that all magnets have a north pole and a south pole.
- I know that two poles of the same type repel each other.
- I know that opposite poles of two magnets attract each other.

3.2 How to use magnets

1 Testing the strength of a magnet

Work with your group.

a. Plan a simple investigation to test the strength of a magnet. Look at the apparatus and equipment in the picture to give you some ideas.

- How will you make sure it is a fair test? ______________________________

  ____

  ____

- What evidence will you look for? ______________________________

  ____

- Write your plan on a separate sheet of paper.

Show your teacher your plan. Then carry out your investigation.

b. How strong is your magnet? Circle your answer on the scale.

1 = very weak   5 = very strong

1 — 2 — 3 — 4 — 5

Why do you say so?

We give the magnet this strength score because

____

____

Hint

We can test the strength of a magnet by measuring the distance between the magnet and a metal object when the object starts to move.

continues on following page …

... continued from previous page

c. Also test some other magnets. How do they compare?

- How will you know which magnet is the strongest from this experiment? ______________________________

____

- Which of your magnets was strongest? Draw a picture of it.

Magnet: ______________________________

Extension

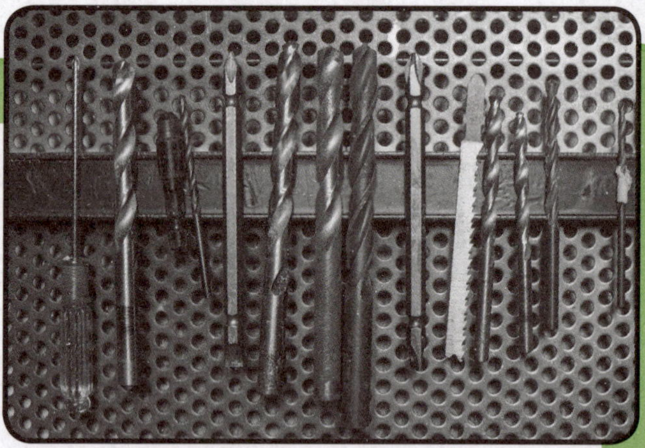

Magnets can be used to hold different objects, such as tools and knives.

Suggest how we can test the strength of these magnets.

Write your plan here.

____

____

____

____

____

____

2 Strong and weak magnets

Your teacher will give you some more magnets to test. They are all of the same type and size.

- One has been handled and stored correctly.
- One has been dropped on the floor.
- One has been stored without keepers.

a. Which magnet do you think will be the strongest?

____

b. Use your plan from Activity 1 to test the strength of these magnets.

- What will you measure? Write it in the top row of the table. Remember to add a unit.
- Repeat the test to make sure your results are reliable.

Type of magnet	______________________		
	Test 1	**Test 2**	**Test 3**
Magnet handled correctly			
Magnet dropped on the floor			
Magnet stored without keepers			

c. Draw a bar chart to show your results. Use the average measurement for each magnet.

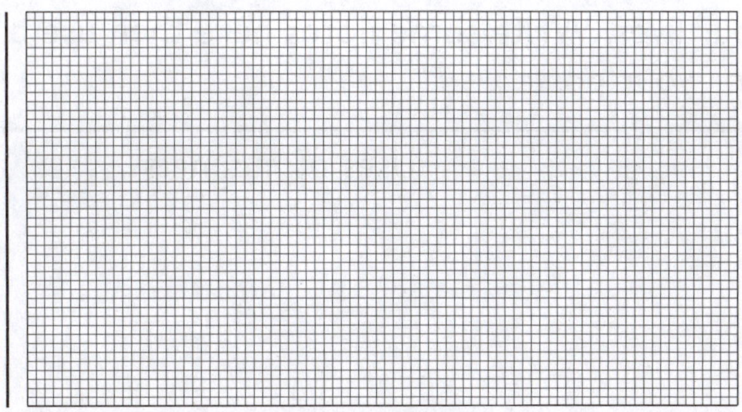

Type of magnet

- Which magnet was the weakest? ______________________
- Which magnet was the strongest? ______________________
- Do your results confirm your prediction? **Yes** **No**

3.3 Uses of magnets

Practising my science language

1 How magnets are used in our world

Your teacher will show you a video about how magnets are used.

a. Write some notes about what you learn from the video.

Magnets are useful in our daily life. Some examples of how magnets are used include:

- ____________________
- ____________________
- ____________________
- ____________________

b. Get into groups. Make a poster about how we use magnets in our lives. Write some notes here then use a big piece of paper for your poster.

Uses of magnets

2 Designing your own use for a magnet

Get into groups. Think about how you can use a magnet to solve one of these problems:

- ☐ Chris knocked over a bowl of screws. They scattered all over the floor. How can he collect the screws easily?
- ☐ Susan plays the flute. She cannot hold her sheet music and play at the same time. How can she use magnets to help her?
- ☐ Jared dropped some coins. They rolled under the fridge. How can he use a magnet to get them out from under the fridge?
- ☐ Monica's mom can never remember where she put her keys. How can Monica use a magnet to help her mom be more organised?

- Tick the problem you want to solve.
- Draw a picture of your solution. Label your drawing.

- Explain to the rest of your class how your idea works.

Extension

Imagine a world without magnets. Write a short description of all the things we would not have. How would this affect our lives?

Checklist

Read each sentence and circle a face for it. Like this:

I understand.

I understand a bit.

I need more help to understand this.

- I know how to handle magnets correctly.
- I can describe how to test the strength of a magnet.
- I can name some uses of magnets in our lives.

Glossary

In your own language, write down what these words mean.

attract

bar magnet

compass

floating magnet

force

horseshoe magnet

keepers

magnet

magnetic

metal

north

poles

repel

south

wand magnet

4.1 Local habitats

Practising my science language

1 Rules for investigating a habitat

a. What should you do to treat plants and animals respectfully?

Here are some suggestions:

- Never tease or scare an animal.
- Collect only as much plant material as you need.
- ______________________________
- ______________________________
- ______________________________
- ______________________________

b. How can you keep safe during your investigation?

Here are some suggestions:

- Always work in a group and stay with your group.
- Do not handle any animal or plant unless you know it is safe to do so.
- ______________________________
- ______________________________
- ______________________________
- ______________________________

Share your ideas as a class.

2 Making a pooter

Get into pairs.

a. Use the materials your teacher gives you to make a pooter.

- Make two holes in the lid of a clear plastic cup or jar.
- Cut one straw somewhat shorter. Put a straw through each hole.
- Wrap a piece of cloth over the bottom end of the shorter straw. Secure it tightly with an elastic band.
- Look at where the straws push through the lid. Seal any gaps around the straws using plasticine.
- Put the lid on the cup or jar. Make sure the straws do not touch the bottom of the cup.

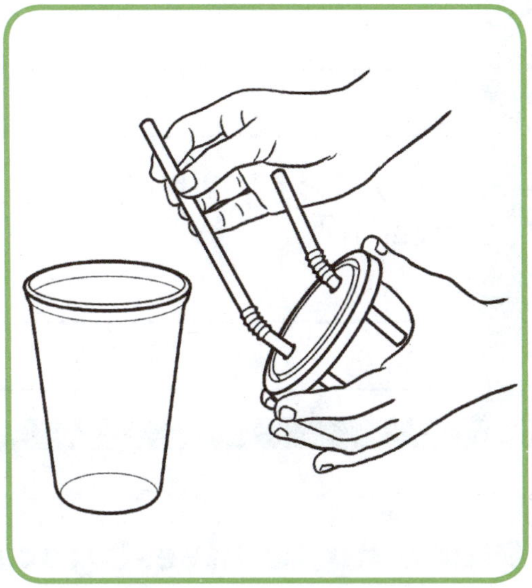

b. Practise using your pooter.

- Put some small beads in a shallow bowl.
- Point the longer straw towards a bead. Then suck on the shorter straw.

What do you see? Explain how the pooter works.

____

____

____

____

____

____

____

____

Extension

What are the advantages of using a pooter?

____

____

Why does the end of the straw you suck through have some cloth over it?

____

____

3 Planning to investigate habitats

Work with a partner.

Imagine you are going to investigate this habitat.

a. Describe the habitat.

____

____

____

____

____

continues on following page …

… continued from previous page

b. What type of animals and plants do you think you will find here? Draw some of your ideas here.

c. What do you want to find out about this habitat?

I want to find out ______________________________

____

d. What equipment will you need to do this investigation?

____

____

e. What measurements will you take?

I will measure ______________________________

____

f. What safety measures should you think about for this investigation?

____

____

4 Investigating habitats

Get into groups. Walk around your school grounds with your teacher.

a. Choose one of the habitats your teacher shows you.

- Describe this habitat.

  We chose the ________________ habitat.

  This habitat has ______________________________

  ____

  ______________________________.

- Draw a picture of the habitat here:

b. Plan how you will investigate the habitat.

- What do you want to find out?

  We want to find out ______________________________

  ______________________________.

- What living things do you expect to find here?

  ____

  ____

- What equipment will you use?

  ____

  ____

- How will you make sure that you work responsibly?

  ____

  ____

continues on following page ...

... continued from previous page

c. Now carry out your investigation.

- How many different plants did you find? ______________________

  Draw a picture of one of them here:

  Describe some of its features.

  ____

  ____

- How many different animals did you find? ____________________

  Draw a picture of one of them here:

  Describe some of its features.

  ____

  ____

5 Making a model habitat

Get into your groups as for Activity 4. Your teacher will give you some materials.

a. Use the materials to make a model of the habitat you investigated earlier.

Ask your teacher to take a picture of your model and print it out. Stick it in the space on the right.

b. Use your model to tell the rest of your class what you found out about the habitat.

Write short notes about what you want to tell the class.

A ______________ habitat

____

____

____

Extension

Think back to one of the habitats you investigated. Write about how it provides food, water, shelter and space for animals and plants to live and breed. ______________________________

____

____

4.2 World habitats

Practising my science language

1 Researching a habitat

Work in your groups.

Tick the habitat you are going to research.

Savannah	☐	Polar ice	☐	Coral reef	☐
Desert	☐	Freshwater lake	☐	Rainforest	☐

Your teacher will give you some resources to research this habitat.

a. Describe the habitat. Circle the correct words:

- The temperature is **warm** / **hot** / **cool** / **cold**.
- It is **often** / **sometimes** / **never** rainy.
- It is **often** / **sometimes** / **never** sunny.
- It is **wet** / **dry** here.
- The temperature changes **a lot** / **only a little** / **not at all** from day to night.

b. Choose five living things (animals and plants) that live here.

- Describe their features.

____

____

____

____

continues on following page ...

… continued from previous page

- Do different animals or plants have any features in common?

  ____

  ____

  ____

  ____

c. Choose one plant and one animal from this habitat.

- How is each one suited to the habitat?

  Plant: ________________

  This plant is suited to the habitat because it ________

  ____

  ____.

  Animal: ________________

  This animal is suited to the habitat because it ________

  ____

  ____.

- How does the habitat provide what the plant and animal need?

  The habitat gives the plant ________________

  ____

  ____.

  The habitat gives the animal ________________

  ____

  ____.

2 Matching animals and plants in a habitat

a. Draw lines to match the animal and plant that belong in the same habitat.

b. Write the name of the habitat next to each pair.

freshwater lake   savannah   polar ice   rainforest
woodland   ocean   mountain

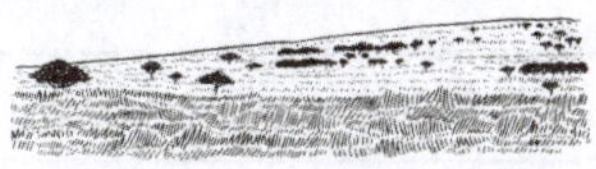

3 Investigating the best conditions for woodlice

Get into groups.

a. Predict which condition will suit woodlice best.
Tick your answer.

Dry dead leaves	☐	Damp dead leaves	☐
Fresh leaves	☐	Open space	☐

b. Make a choice chamber like the one in the picture in the Student Book.

- Divide the Petri dish into four quarters. Put one type of material in each quarter. Leave one quarter clear.
- Place ten woodlice in the choice chamber and carefully replace the lid.
- Count the number of woodlice in each quarter after 15 minutes. Record your results in the table below.

Condition in choice chamber	Number of woodlice found after 15 minutes
Open space	
Dry dead leaves	
Damp dead leaves	
Fresh leaves	

c. Draw a bar graph of your results on the axes provided.

d. Was your prediction correct?

Yes **No**

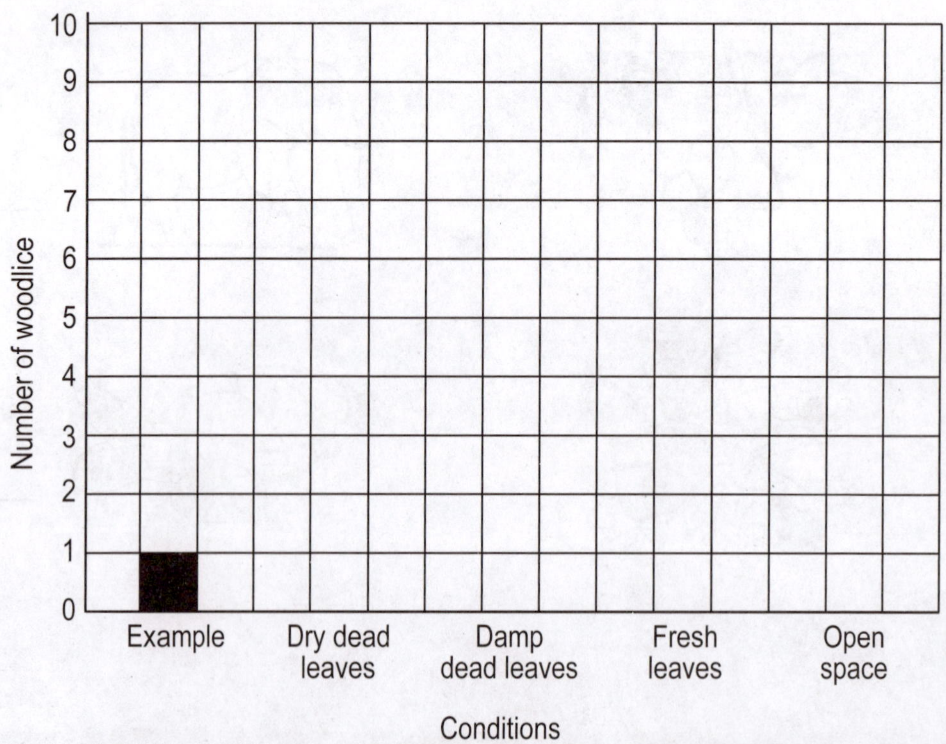

Extension

Look at the woodland habitat on page 75 of your Student Book.

a. Imagine a new animal that would be at home here.

Draw what you think it would look like.

b. Think of a name for this new animal. ________________

c. What features make the animal suited to this habitat?

____

____

____

Hint

Think about what the animal might eat.

Think about how it will move.

Think about the conditions in this habitat.

Think about threats in this habitat.

Checklist

I understand.

I understand a bit.

I need more help to understand this.

Read each sentence and circle a face for it. Like this:

- I can describe what a habitat is.
- I know how to investigate a habitat responsibly.
- I can name different local and world habitats.
- I can name some animals and plants that live in a specific habitat.
- I know that plants and animals are suited to their habitats.

4.3 Identifying animals and plants

1 Describing animals

Get into pairs. Look at the pictures on page 77 of your Student Book.

a. Write down the main features of each animal. An example has been done for each one.

Animal 1	**Animal 2**
It has a tail.	It has a beak.

b. Now turn these features into questions that can be answered with "yes" or "no". For example: "Does it have a tail?"

Write your questions here.

Animal 1: ______________________

____

____

____

____

Animal 2: ______________________

____

____

____

____

2 What am I?

Get into pairs. Your teacher will give you picture cards, some beads and a small jar.

a. Keep the cards face down. Let your partner choose one of the cards.

b. Ask your partner questions to find out what animal is shown.

Put a bead in the jar each time you ask a question.

The first question I asked was: ______________________________

____.

The last question I asked was: ______________________________

____.

c. How many questions did it take to get the answer?

I had to ask ______________ *questions to find out that the card showed a* ______________.

Practising my science language

3 Working with a simple identification key

Look at the pictures on page 80 of the Student Book.

a. Describe the features of each animal.

- Lion: ______________________________

  ____

  ____

- Tiger: ______________________________

  ____

  ____

continues on following page …

… continued from previous page

- Impala: ______________________________

____

____

- Giraffe: ______________________________

____

____

b. Complete the identification key. Write the name of each animal in the correct space.

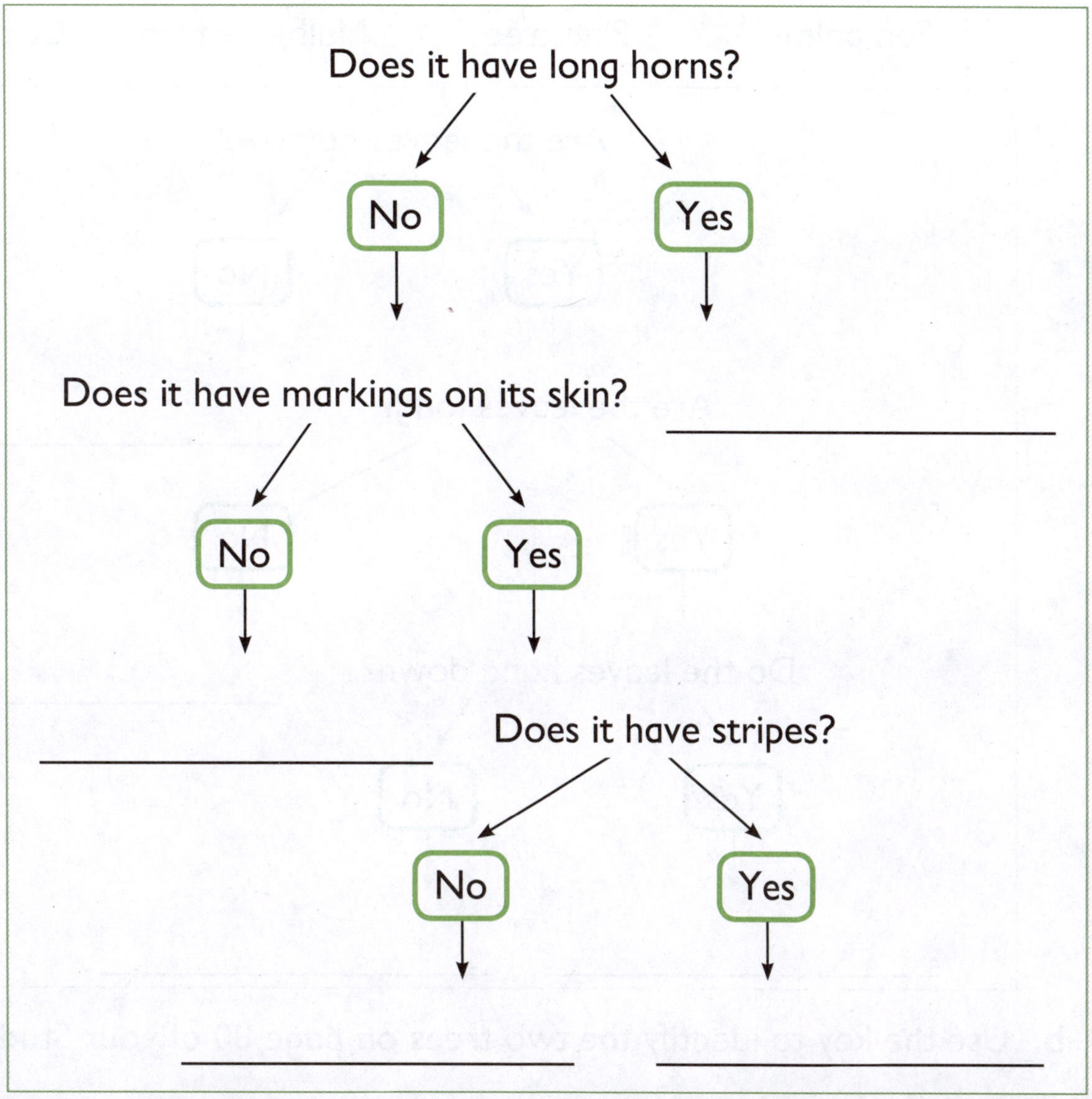

4 An identification key for plants

We can use identification keys for plants too.

a. Look at the pictures of the leaves of different trees. Complete the identification key.

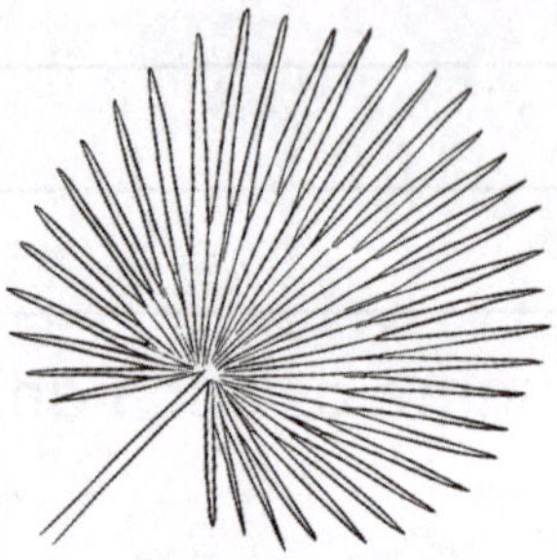

Fan palm

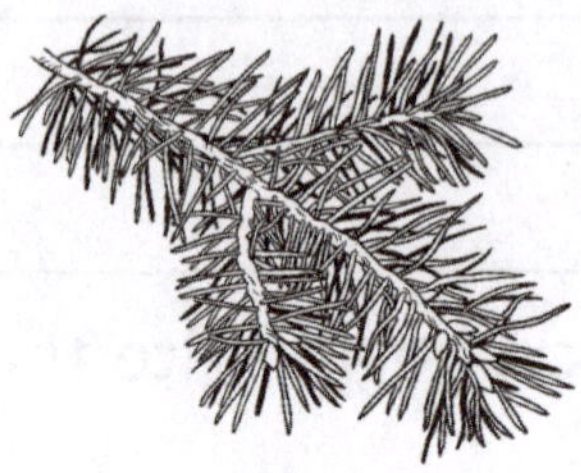

Pine tree

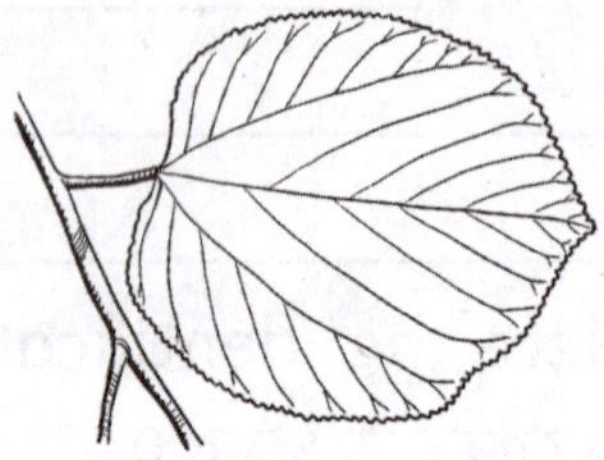

Mulberry tree

Coconut palm

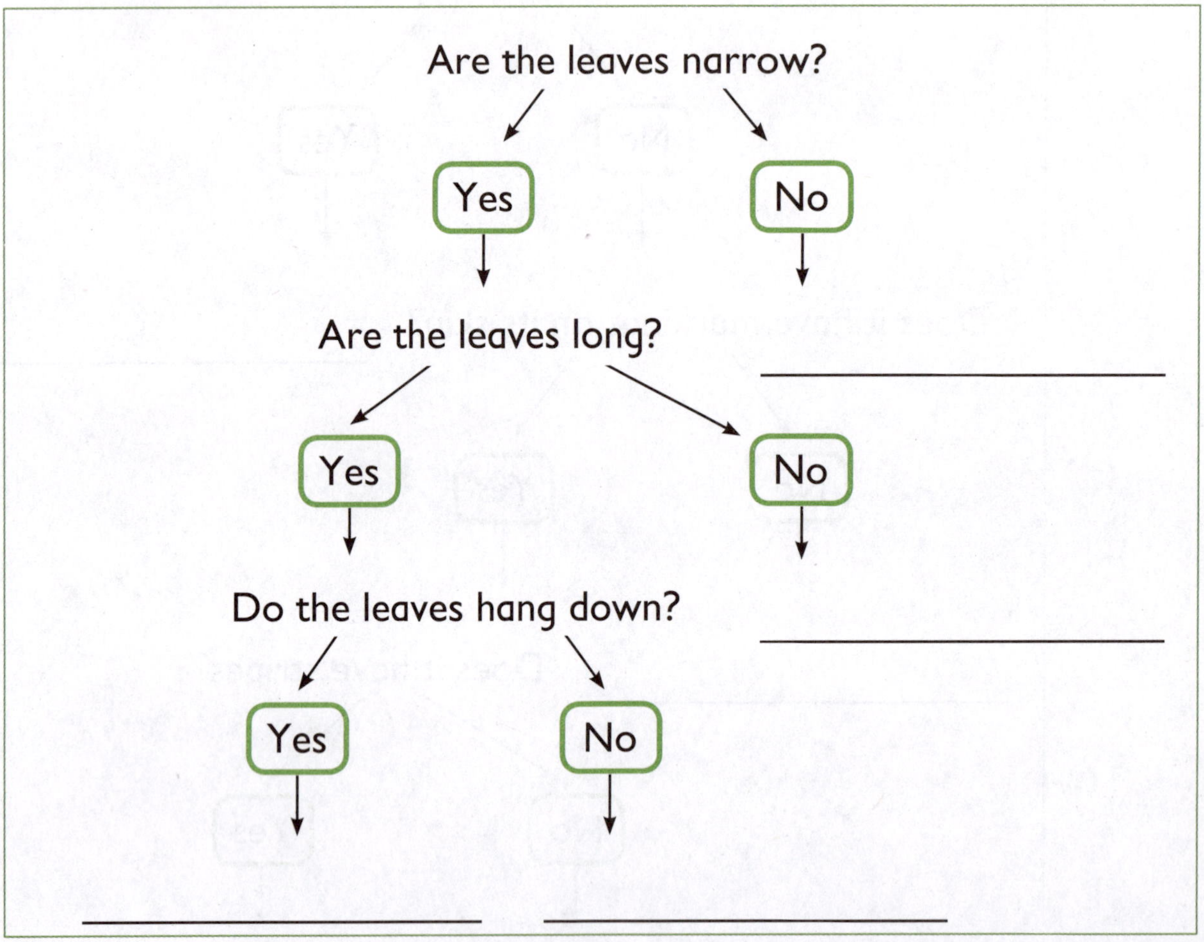

b. Use the key to identify the two trees on page 80 of your Student Book.

Tree 1: ____________________

Tree 2: ____________________

Extension

Jayesh wants to identify the snakes on page 81 of the Student Book.

He asked these questions to make an identification key:

- Is the pattern stripey?
- Does the snake have a pattern?
- Are some of the stripes yellow?

a. Write each question in the correct space in the diagram.

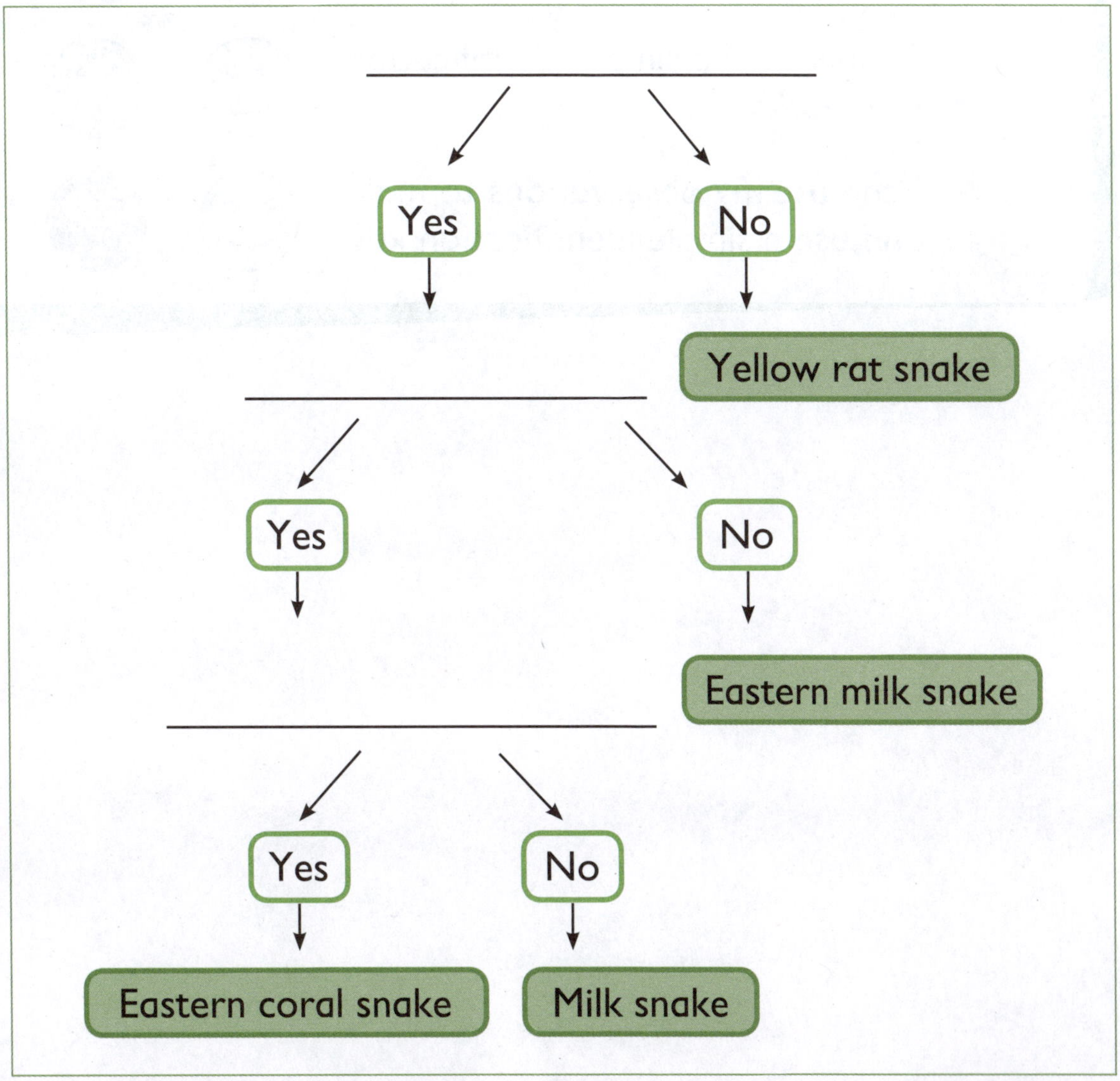

b. Now use the key to identify the snakes shown in your Student Book.

A: ____________________ B: ____________________

C: ____________________ D: ____________________

Checklist

I understand.

I understand a bit.

I need more help to understand this.

Read each sentence and circle a face for it. Like this:

- I can describe the features of plants and animals.
- I know how a simple identification key works.
- I can use my observations to make and use a simple identification key.

4.4 How human activity affects the environment

1 Researching local developments

a. Find a new development in your area. Use newspapers or the internet, or walk around to find out more about it.

Answer the questions about the new development.

- What is the development? ______________________________

  ____

- What used to be in the space before?

  Before the development took place there was ______________________________

  ____

  ____

b. How are local habitats affected?

- What animals and plants might have lived there before?

  ____

  ____

- What will happen to them because of this development?

  ____

  ____

c. What do you think are the advantages and disadvantages of this development?

- I think some advantages are that ______________________________

  ______________________________.

- I think some disadvantages are that ______________________________

  ______________________________.

Practising my **science language**

2 Making our voice heard

a. Read the letter Tara wrote to her town's planning officer.

Dear Mr Boulder,

I am writing to you about the plans for a new shopping centre in place of Grassy Green Park. My friends and I go to the park every day. If this becomes a shopping centre we will not have anywhere to play. We see many other people from our town there as well. Everyone enjoys relaxing on the lawns, having a picnic or admiring the beautiful gardens.

Our school did a recent habitat study of the park. We discovered many different animals that live there, including mice, foxes and badgers. We also identified three different families of nesting birds. We counted many different trees and some of the older people in town say that the trees were already there when they were children. The trees must be almost a hundred years old!

What will happen to these plants and animals if a shopping centre is built? Everyone at our school hopes you will reconsider the development.

Yours faithfully,

Tara Walsh

continues on following page ...

... continued from previous page

b. Answer these questions.

- What is Tara worried about?

  ____

  ____

- Why do the townspeople need the park?

  ____

  ____

- Why do the plants and animals need the park?

  ____

  ____

Extension

How can scientists work with planners to make sure that animals, plants and humans can live together?

____

____

____

____

____

____

____

____

____

3 Combatting plastic pollution

Get into pairs.

Do some research to find out what people are doing to prevent or solve the problem of plastic pollution.

- What did you find out?

  During our research we found out about ______________________

  ____.

  This involves ______________________________

  ____.

- Draw a picture about your findings.

Extension

Imagine you have been asked to design something to collect plastic from the ocean.

a. Write some notes about how your idea works.

____

____

____

____

____

b. Draw and label your design.

4.5 Environmental challenges for the Earth

1 Impact of natural disasters

Your teacher will show you some video clips about natural disasters.

After each video, discuss the impact of the disaster on the local people and habitats. Also talk about how people respond.

Write short notes about each video clip here.

- Name of disaster: ______________________________

____

____

- Name of disaster: ______________________________

____

____

- Name of disaster: ______________________________

____

____

- Name of disaster: ______________________________

____

____

- Name of disaster: ______________________________

____

____

- Name of disaster: ______________________________

____

____

2 Impact of human-made disasters

Watch the video clip about a human-made disaster.

Name of the disaster: ______________________________

Now answer these questions.

a. How does the disaster affect people's lives?

____

____

____

For how long are they affected?

____

What are the main problems?

____

____

____

b. How does the disaster affect the environment?

____

____

____

Do the environmental effects last for long or only for a short time?

____

c. What can people do to manage the environmental effects?

____

____

____

d. How can a similar disaster be prevented in future?

____

____

____

Practising my

science language

3 Hurricane Sandy

a. Read the case study about Hurricane Sandy below.

Case study: Hurricane Sandy

A hurricane is a very powerful storm that develops over tropical oceans. It brings very strong winds and heavy rain, and can cause lots of damage if it reaches land.

In October 2012, a strong hurricane hit parts of the Caribbean and the east coast of the United States. It was called Hurricane Sandy. Winds of 120 – 130 km/h were recorded. This is about the speed at which you travel on a highway. Heavy rain caused flooding over large areas and many crop fields, pastures and animal habitats were destroyed. Trees were uprooted, power lines fell over and telecommunications were lost. More than 250 people died during this event.

Many people had to leave their homes. Almost 700 000 homes were damaged or destroyed. There were power failures in many areas of cities such as New York and Washington and many businesses had to close. Flights were grounded and railways, roads and bridges could not be used because of flooding or damage. The hurricane cost the United States government about $60 billion.

b. Answer these questions.

- What is a hurricane? ______________________________
  ____
- Where did this event occur?
  ____
- When did this event occur? ______________________________
- Why do you think this event was classified as a disaster?
  ____

continues on following page ...

… continued from previous page

- How were people affected? ______________________

____

____

- How was the environment affected? ______________________

____

____

- How do you think you would have responded if you were there? ______________________

____

____

Extension

Research one of these natural disasters:

- The earthquake in Lombok Island, Indonesia, in 2018
- The tsunami in Thailand in December 2004
- The volcanic eruption in Hawaii in 2018

I am going to do research about:

____

______________________.

What did you find out? You can write some notes or paste a picture of what you found here.

4.6 Promoting environmental awareness

1 Monitoring your school environment

Get into groups.

a. Choose one of the focus areas listed in your Student Book.

b. Do some research about how environmentally aware your school is. You can interview people, take measurements or take pictures to collect some evidence.

c. Record your findings in the worksheet your teacher gives you.

Extension

Prepare a presentation for your school assembly. Write your notes below.

a. Outline all the things your school is doing well.

b. Suggest some things you could do to improve the environment around your school.

c. Think about how you can monitor the changes.

Checklist

I understand.

I understand a bit.

I need more help to understand this.

Read each sentence and circle a face for it. Like this:

- I can describe the impact of local developments on habitats.
- I can name some natural disasters and some caused by humans.
- I understand the effects of environmental disasters.
- I can describe how we can respond to environmental disasters.
- I can help to care for the environment at school.

Glossary

In your own language, write down what these words mean:

animals

brick wall

creatures

development

disaster

earthquakes

environment

features

habitat

identification key

leaf pile

litter

local

log pile

meadow

natural disasters

Glossary

oil slick

plants

pollution

pond

pooter

recycle

stones

tsunami

volcano

woodland

5.1 Making circuits

1 Making a circuit

a. Construct a working circuit using the following components:

- one cell
- a lamp
- a lamp holder
- two wires
- two connectors

Draw the circuit in the box.

b. Does the lamp light up?

Yes **No**

Explain your observation.

____

____

____

2 How does adding cells affect a circuit?

a. Construct the circuits shown in your Student Book. Use the components your teacher gives you.

b. What happens when you add more cells to the circuit?

____

c. What have you discovered?

____

____

____

Extension

Batteries come in all shapes and sizes.

Write the name of a device in which these batteries can be used.

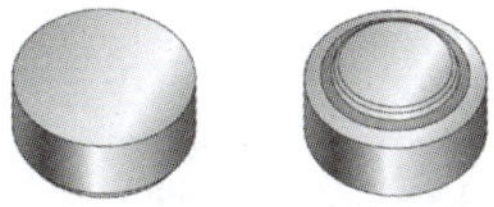

____

____

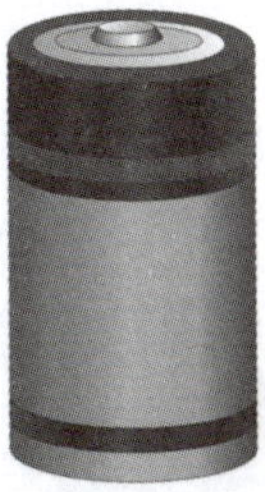

____

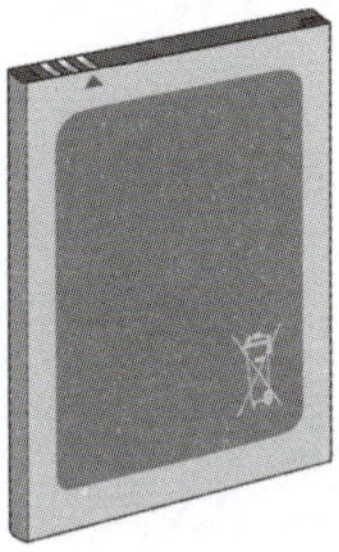

____

3 How does adding lamps affect a circuit?

a. Set up the two circuits shown in the diagram.

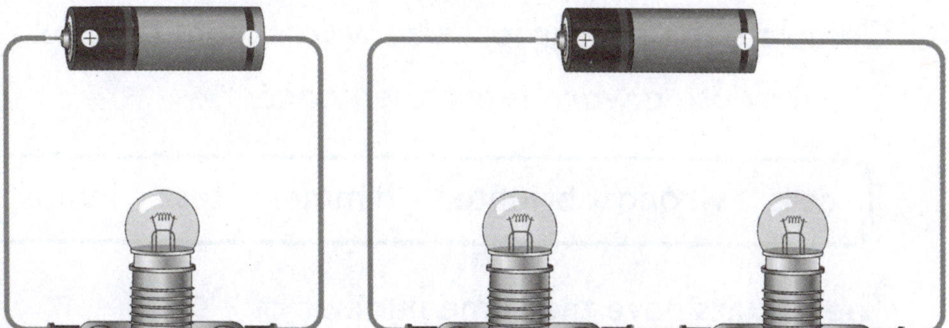

b. What did you observe when you added another lamp to the circuit?

____

____

c. What do you predict will happen if you add a third lamp?

The more lamps we add to a simple circuit, the **dimmer / brighter** they will be.

Practising my

science language

4 Making predictions

Here are some circuits.

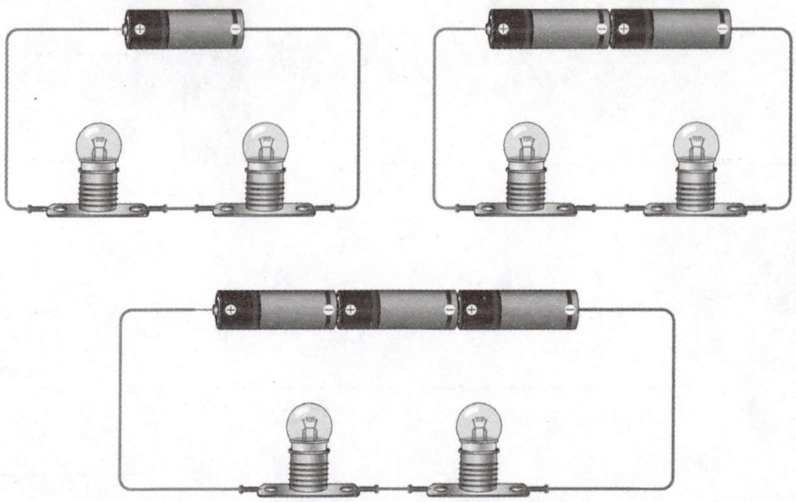

a. How will the brightness of the lamps compare between the circuits? Colour in the lamps to show your prediction.

b. Construct the circuits to test your prediction. What did you find out?

Complete the paragraph. Use words from the box.

You may use a word more than once.

cells	wrong	brighter	dimmer	test	lamps	right

The circuits have the same number of ________________, but a different number of ________________. We predicted that the lamps will be ________________ in a circuit with one cell than in a circuit with three cells. We constructed the circuit to ________________ our prediction. Our test showed that adding more ________________ to a circuit makes the lamps shine ________________. We found out that our prediction was ________________.

5 Components of circuits

Your teacher will give you a buzzer and a motor, together with other components to make a circuit.

a. Construct a complete circuit using one cell and a motor.

- What do you observe?

  ___

- Break the circuit. Add another cell to the circuit to make a battery.

  What is the effect on the motor when you complete the circuit again?

  ___

- Break the circuit. Attach a small propeller to the motor spindle.

  Complete the circuit again.

  What do you observe? Draw a picture to show your answer.

b. Construct a complete circuit using one cell and a buzzer.

- What do you observe?

  ___

- How can you use a circuit that includes a buzzer?

  ___

  ___

Extension

a. What components can you see in the picture?

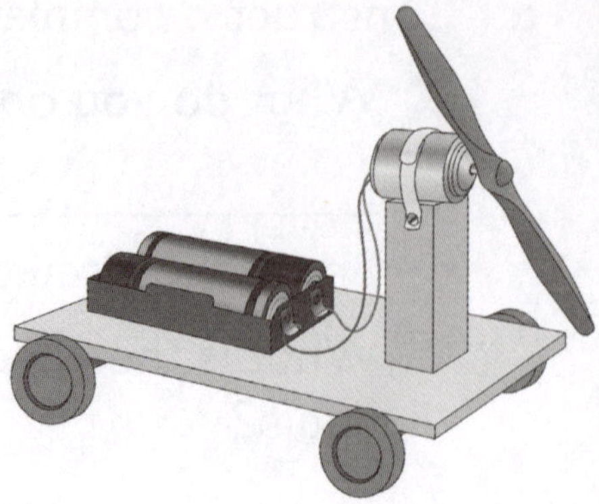

b. What will happen if the circuit is switched on?

Checklist

Read each sentence and circle a face for it. Like this:

- I understand.
- I understand a bit.
- I need more help to understand this.

- I can name some circuit components.
- I know how to construct a circuit.
- I understand what happens when more cells and components are added to a circuit.

5.2 Switches

1 Comparing circuits

a. Predict whether these circuits will work.

- Tick the ones you think will work.
- Make a cross next to the ones you think will not work.

A
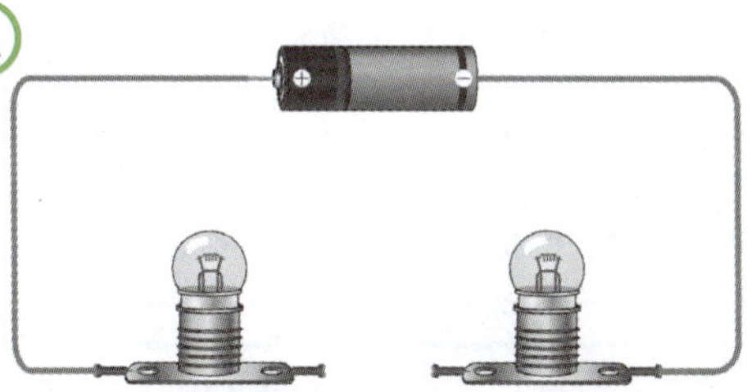
☐

B
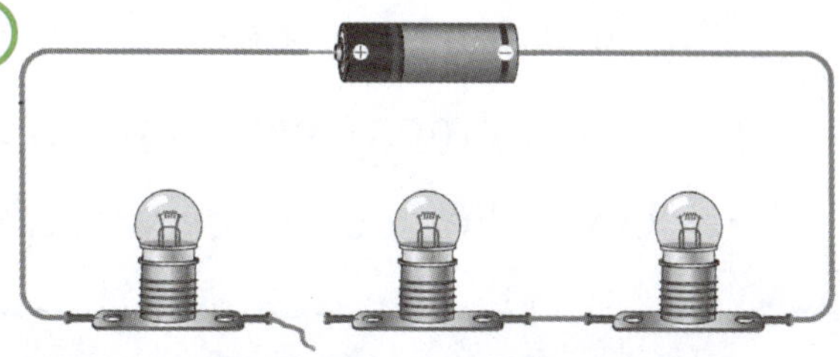
☐

C
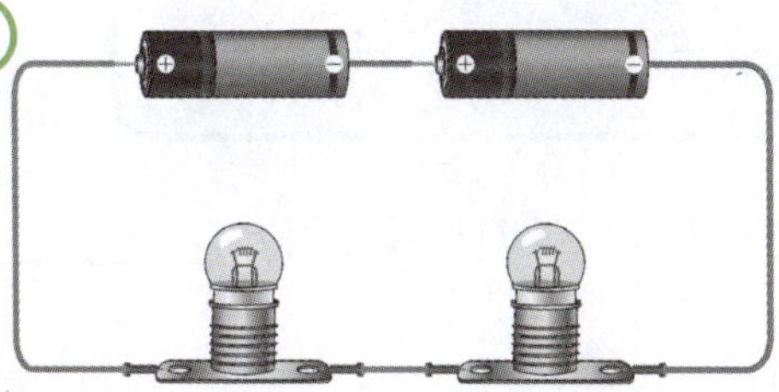
☐

D
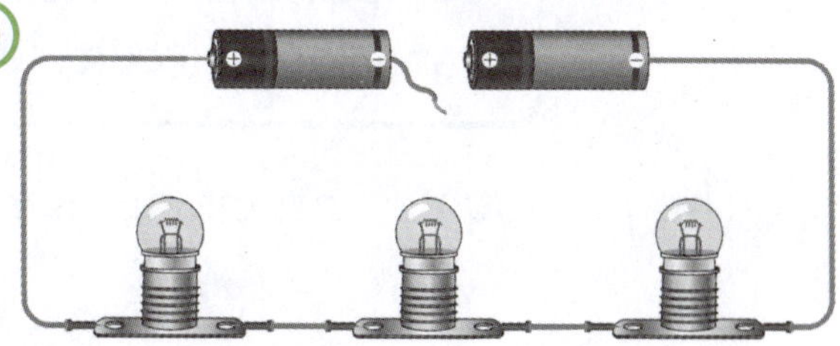
☐

b. Make each circuit in turn. Were your predictions right or wrong? Circle your answer in the table.

For circuit A	my prediction was	**right / wrong**
For circuit B		**right / wrong**
For circuit C		**right / wrong**
For circuit D		**right / wrong**

c. What is your conclusion?

A lamp will ____________ if the circuit is working. A circuit has to be ____________ to work. If there is a ____________ in the circuit, it will not work. It does not matter at what point the ____________ occurs.

Practising my

science language

2 Explaining how a flashlight works

Get into pairs. Look at the design of a simple flashlight.

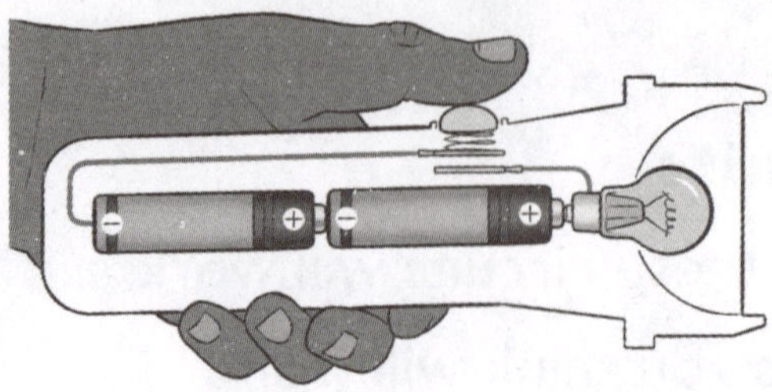

Write a short paragraph to explain how the flashlight works. The first part has been done for you.

- Use as many words from the box as you can.
- Underline each key word you use.

component	battery	wire	complete	circuit
working circuit	break	switch	cell	lamp

The flashlight contains an electrical circuit. It consists of ____________

____

____

____

____

Extension

Go on a tour of your school.

a. How many different items can you find with a switch? ____________

b. Draw a picture of some of the items on a piece of paper. Show how the switches look.

Safety

Be careful:
Do not touch any of the electrical items. They may be hot.

3 Making your own switch

Get into groups.

a. Follow the instructions to make your own switch and use it in a circuit.

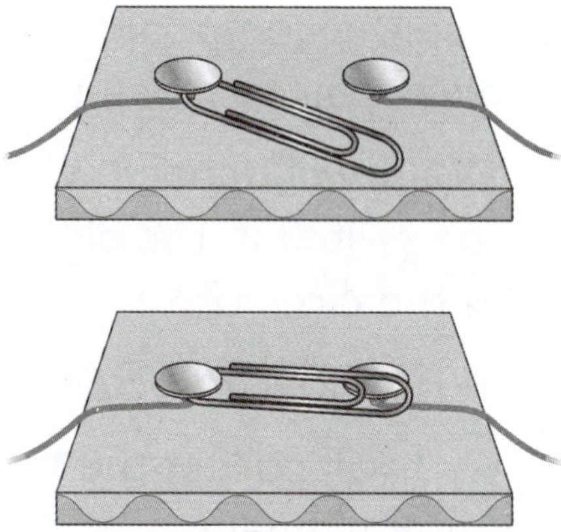

- Push a drawing pin through the bend of a paper clip. Then press the drawing pin into a piece of cardboard.
- Press another drawing pin into the cardboard. Check that the free end of the paper clip will rest on the head of the drawing pin.

b. Now connect the switch into a circuit. Use the components that your teacher gives you.

- Move the paper clip to touch the drawing pin. What happens to the lamp?

  ____

- Is the switch on or off? Why do you say so?

  I know the switch is **on** / **off** because ____________________

  ____.

- Move the switch back to its previous position. What happens now?

  ____

  ____

c. Test the switch with different components, like a buzzer and then a motor.

What do you observe? Does the switch work in the same way with each component?

When I connect the buzzer in the circuit and close the switch, __________

____.

When I connect the motor in the circuit and close the switch, __________

____.

Closing the switch turns the components **on** / **off**.

4 Switching off some components

Get into groups.

a. Use the components your teacher gives you to make this circuit.

b. What will happen when you place the switch in the different positions in the circuit?

Write how you can find out here.

- I will collect the following equipment:

  ____

  ____

- First I will ______________________________

  ____

  ____

- Then I will ______________________________

  ____

  ____

- Finally I will ______________________________

  ____

  ____

c. Now connect the switches as planned. Present your results and describe what happens in each case.

____

____

____

____

Extension

Try to make switches with some other items your teacher gives you.

a. Which items make the best switch?

____

b. Design a switch that you can release quickly using one of these items. Draw your design here.

Checklist

I understand.

I understand a bit.

I need more help to understand this.

Read each sentence and circle a face for it. Like this:

- I can describe what happens when there is a break in a circuit.
- I know what the job of a switch is.
- I can explain why a switch is useful in a circuit.
- I can describe how to make a simple switch.

5.3 Models for describing circuits

1 A human circuit model

Work as a class. Make a human circuit model as in the picture on page 103 of your Student Book.

Your teacher will represent the cell.

- Someone will be a circuit component, like a buzzer.
- The rest of you will be the energy particles in the circuit.
- Walk around in the circle when your teacher says "Switch on!" Stop when your teacher says "Switch off!"

Complete the paragraph to describe what the model shows about how electricity works.

buzzer	lamp	sound	circuit	energy
light up	sweet	component	motor	turn

We walked in a circle to represent a ________________. Our teacher was the cell. One learner was a component. We chose the component to be a ________________. The cell provides ________________ for the components in a circuit. We each carried a cup. When we passed the teacher, she put a ________________ into our cups. This represented energy. Every time we passed the component, we gave it our sweets so that it could ________________. When we passed the teacher again, she put a new sweet into our cups. This meant we could keep giving energy to the ________________ to work.

Extension

A doll's house is a model of a real house.

a. In what ways is it a good model? ______________________

____

b. What are the limitations of this model? ______________________

____

Practising my science language

2 Adapting a model for different circuits

Get into groups.

a. How will you change the model you made in Activity 1 to represent the following circuits?

- For a circuit with two cells instead of one, we will ______________________

  ______________________.

- For a circuit with a lamp and a buzzer, we will ______________________

  ______________________.

- For a circuit with a switch, we will ______________________

  ______________________.

b. Demonstrate your new models to the rest of your class.

5.4 Safety with electricity at home

1 Safety at home

Your teacher will show you a video about using electricity safely at home.

Write some notes here to remind you of the important points.

____

____

____

____

____

____

____

2 Making a safety poster

Get into groups. Look at the posters your teacher shows you.

a. What makes a poster eye-catching?

____

____

____

____

____

b. Design your own poster about safety with electricity. It should help people at home.

continues on following page …

... continued from previous page

c. Look at the poster from one of the other groups.

- Do you think it is effective? **Yes** **No**
- Why do you say so? Write some notes here to share with the rest of the class. ______________________

____

____

Extension

When Nissa uses her hairdryer, she can touch the black cable and not feel any shock. Can you explain why? ______________________

____

____

Checklist

I understand.

I understand a bit.

I need more help to understand this.

Read each sentence and circle a face for it. Like this:

- I can describe a model that shows how a circuit works.
- I can explain how parts of a model are like the real thing, but others are not.
- I can describe how to change a model to show different circuits.
- I can identify situations where electricity is being used dangerously.
- I can describe how to be safe with electricity.

Glossary

In your own language, write down what these words mean:

battery

break

buzzer

cell

circuit

complete

components

connector

crocodile clip

current

danger

electricity

flow

lamp

lamp holder

mains electricity

Glossary

model

motor

particles

safety

switch

voltage

wire

working circuit

6.1 Exploring how sounds are made

1 Making sounds

Your teacher has set up some sound stations around the room. With your partner, go to three stations. Make some sounds with the things you find at each station. Answer the questions.

dull	sharp	loud	ringing	shrill	clicking
deep	rising	melodious	creaky	ticking	squeaky
clanging	twanging	gritty	grainy	pounding	soft

We went to station ______________.

a. What did you do to make the sound?

____

____

b. What did you see when you made the sound?

I saw ____.

c. What was the sound like? You can choose words from the box or use your own.

The sound was ____.

We went to station ______________.

a. What did you do to make the sound?

____

____

b. What did you see when you made the sound?

I saw ____.

continues on following page …

... continued from previous page

c. What was the sound like? You can choose words from the box or use your own.

The sound was ______________________________.

We went to station __________.

a. What did you do to make the sound? ______________________________

____

b. What did you see when you made the sound?

I saw ______________________________.

c. What was the sound like? You can choose words from the box or use your own.

The sound was ______________________________.

Extension

Look at the pictures. Which instrument matches the sound you heard at each station?

The ______________ makes the same sound as the object in Station **A** / **B** / **C** / **D** / **E**.

The ______________ makes the same sound as the object in Station **A** / **B** / **C** / **D** / **E**.

The ______________ makes the same sound as the object in Station **A** / **B** / **C** / **D** / **E**.

violin

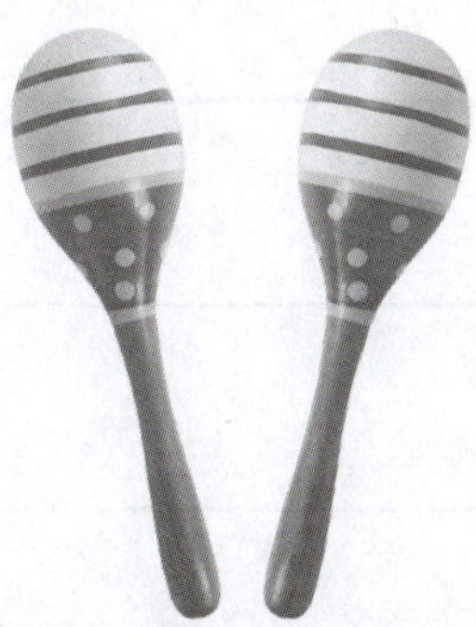
maracas

triangle
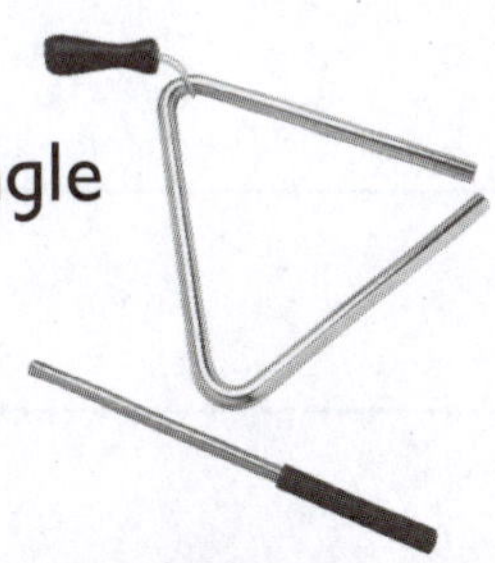

drum

thumb piano

2 Good vibrations

Look at the pictures of Jessica and Simone in your Student Book.

a. Which instrument do they each play?

Jessica plays the _______________.

Simone plays the _______________.

b. What does Jessica do to make her instrument vibrate?

____

____

c. What does Simone do to make her instrument vibrate?

____

____

d. Do the instruments sound the same? Circle your answer. **Yes** **No**

3 Measuring sound

Get into groups. Go on a tour of your school. Listen to some sounds.

a. Measure the loudness of different sounds using a sound level meter. Record the values in the table.

An example has been done for you.

Source of sound	Loudness in decibels (dB)
playground sounds	70 dB

continues on following page …

... continued from previous page

b. What was the loudest sound you heard? ___

What was the softest sound you heard? ___

c. What trend do you see? Choose the right word in each sentence.

For loud sounds, we recorded a **high** / **low** value with the sound level meter. For soft sounds, we recorded a **high** / **low** value.

Practising my science language

4 What happens when you move away from a sound?

Get into groups. Plan an investigation to find out how a sound changes with distance.

a. Describe how you will set up the investigation. Complete these sentences to help you.

- We are going to measure ___.
- We are going to use the following equipment: ___
- To make a sound, we are going to ___.
- To change the distance from the sound, we will ___.
- To make the test fair, we will ___.

b. What are the variables in the investigation?

___

c. What result do you predict?

___

Extension

Ask your partner to play a musical instrument at different volumes.

a. Predict the loudness of the sound in decibels and record it in the table.

b. Then measure the loudness of the sound and record your result.

c. How close were your predictions? Circle your answers.

	Predicted loudness (dB)	Measured loudness (dB)	How close were you?
Sound 1			Close / Not close
Sound 2			Close / Not close
Sound 3			Close / Not close

Checklist

I understand.

I understand a bit.

I need more help to understand this.

Read each sentence and circle a face for it. Like this:

- I know that vibrations are the source of sound.
- I can say how different objects, including musical instruments, produce vibrations.
- I can describe how to measure the loudness of a sound.
- I know that loudness is measured in decibels.
- I can investigate how the loudness of a sound changes with distance.

6.2 Sound all around

1 Can sound travel through solids?

For this activity you need a coat hanger and some string.

a. Make a simple apparatus as shown in the picture.

b. How can you use the apparatus to test whether sound travels through solids?

____

____

____

c. Describe your observations. Can you explain what happens?

____

____

____

2 Listening to a sound through a liquid

Get into pairs.

a. Cut off the bottom half of the bottle as shown in the picture. This will be your listening device.

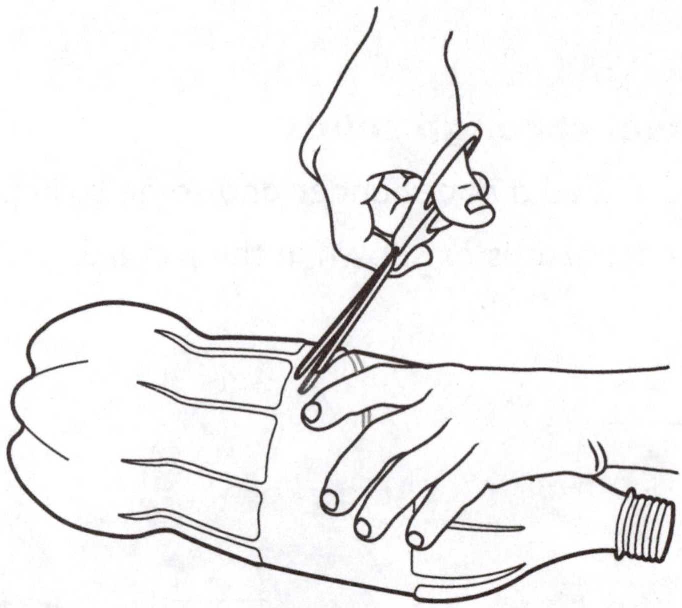

b. Ask your partner to tap two spoons together in the air.

How does it sound? Tick your answer.

- ☐ The sound is very soft. I can hardly hear it.
- ☐ The sound is clear enough for me to hear it.
- ☐ The sound is so loud it hurts my ears.

c. Put the listening device into the bowl of water. Now ask your partner to tap the spoons together under the water. Listen through the device.

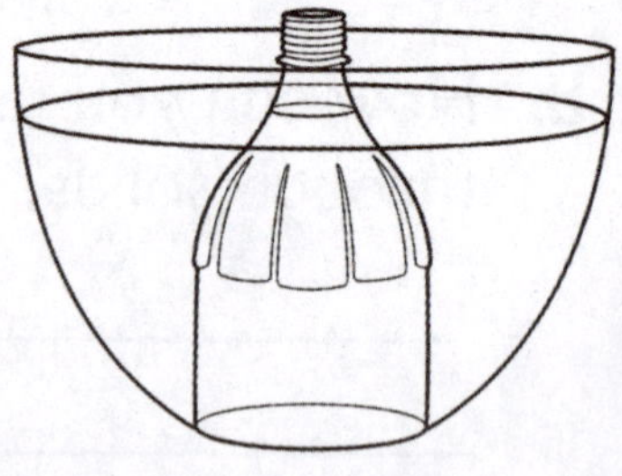

How is the sound different now? Circle your answer.

The sound is **louder / softer** now.

d. What can you conclude from this investigation?

____

____

3 Investigating how sound travels

Someone in your class will go outside and make a loud sound.

Complete the diagram to show how the sound travels from its source to your ears.

Source of sound → ________________ → ________________ → ________________ → My ears

4 Making a string telephone

Get into pairs. Your teacher will give you two paper cups and a length of string.

a. Make a string telephone like in the diagram.

b. Take it in turns to test your telephone. Say a sequence of numbers.

- What numbers did your partner say?

  ____

- How well does the telephone work?

  I think the telephone works **very well** / **not well at all** because

  ____

  ____

c. Explain how the telephone works. Think about what you know about materials and vibrations.

____

____

____

6.3 How to block sounds

Practising my science language

1 Measuring the loudness of a sound through different solids

a. Work as a class. Plan an investigation to find out how different materials affect the loudness of a sound. Choose the right options in these questions to help you.

- What will your variables be?

  ☐ Type of material ☐ Distance ☐ Loudness

- What should you do to make this a fair test?

  ☐ Keep all the conditions the same every time.

  ☐ Change one variable at a time, but keep all the other conditions the same.

- How will you present your results? You can choose more than one method.

  ☐ In a table ☐ As a written paragraph

  ☐ As a labelled drawing ☐ As a graph

- Now write your plan here.

  First we will ______________________________

  ______________________________.

  Next we will ______________________________

  ______________________________.

continues on following page ...

… continued from previous page

Then we will ____

____.

We will measure and record ___________________________

____.

b. Carry out your investigation. Complete the paragraph to explain your observations.

wave	sand	easier	air	louder	material
gas	harder	particles	softer	cotton wool	wood

Sound travels as a __________ of energy. As the energy moves through a __________, the energy is transferred to its __________. Sound does not travel as well through sand or __________ as it does through __________. The sand and cotton wool trap some __________. We know that the particles in a __________ are not as closely packed together as in a solid. This explains why we recorded a __________ sound through __________ than through wood.

2 Investigating how to block sound

Get into groups. Imagine you have been asked to design a soundproof music room.

Your teacher will give you some materials.

a. Plan how you can investigate which material will be best for a soundproof room.

Describe the setup for your investigation here. You can write a paragraph or draw a labelled picture.

continues on following page …

... continued from previous page

b. Tick three materials you want to test.

- [ ] Foam
- [ ] A thick towel
- [ ] Paper
- [ ] Aluminium foil
- [ ] Thin plastic
- [ ] Polystyrene

Why do you think these materials will be suitable for soundproofing?

____

____

Checklist

I understand.

I understand a bit.

I need more help to understand this.

Read each sentence and circle a face for it. Like this:

- I know that sound travels from its source to our ears.
- I know that sound needs a material to travel through.
- I can compare how sound travels through solids, liquids and gases.
- I can explain why sound travels better through some materials than others.
- I discovered that some materials are better than others at blocking sound.

6.4 Investigating pitch

1 Different instruments, different sounds

Select one instrument from the photos on page 123 in the Student Book.

Describe to your partner the different sounds that can come from the instrument. An example has been done for you.

If you pluck the longest string of the harp, you can make a low-pitched sound.

____

____

____

____

2 Can you tell a high pitch from a low pitch?

Get into pairs. Listen to the sounds your teacher plays.

- If the sound is high, jump up.
- If the sound is low, sit down.

Draw a tally line in the chart for each sound you hear.

Low sounds	High sounds

Extension

You now have four words to describe sounds:

- "high" and "low" for pitch
- "loud" and "soft" for volume.

Choose the best combination of words to describe these sounds. The first one has been done for you.

The crash of cymbals	loud, high
The sound of thunder	
A whisper to a friend	
Your heartbeat	
Distant birdsong	

3 Making your own music

Get into groups. Each of you should choose a glass or a bottle as an instrument.

a. Try different ways to make a sound with your instrument.

I chose a ____________________.

I can make a sound with it by ______________________________.

If I add some water, the sound is ______________________________.

b. Put together a pattern of sounds in your group to play some music.

Practising my

science language

4 Investigating sounds with different liquids

Get into your glass band again. Use the same instrument as before. Use cooking oil rather than water this time.

a. Try to recreate the same pattern of pitches from before.

b. Write your observations here. ______________________

____

____

Hint

Think about these ideas:

- Is it hard to get the same pitch?
- Did you have to use more or less oil than water?
- Did you have to go faster or slower?

Checklist

Read each sentence and circle a face for it. Like this:

I understand.

I understand a bit.

I need more help to understand this.

- I can identify the sounds of different instruments.
- I know that "high" and "low" describe the pitch of a sound.
- I can recognise different pitches.
- I can make high, low, loud and soft sounds.

Glossary

In your own language, write down what these words mean:

brass

decibels

high

loud

low

material

musical instruments

noise

percussion

pitch

prevent

soft

sound

sound level meter

sound wave

string

Glossary

travel

voice box

tuning

volume

tuning fork

woodwind

vibrate